CLASSIC WALKS IN THE
Yorkshire Dales

by Walt Unsworth

 The Oxford Illustrated Press

The Oxford Illustrated Press

© Walt Unsworth, 1989

ISBN 0 946609 87 X

Published by:
The Oxford Illustrated Press Limited, Haynes Publishing
Group, Sparkford, Nr Yeovil, Somerset BA22 7JJ, England.
Haynes Publications Inc., 861 Lawrence Drive, Newbury
Park, California 91320, USA.

Printed in England by:
J.H. Haynes & Co Limited, Sparkford, Nr Yeovil, Somerset.

British Library Cataloguing in Publication Data
Unsworth, Walt, 1928-
   Classic walks in the Yorkshire Dales.
   1. North Yorkshire. National parks. Yorkshire Dales
National Park. Visitors' guides
   I. Title
   914.28'404858

   ISBN 0-946609-87-X

Library of Congress Catalog Card Number
89-84454

CONTENTS

Introduction

The Yorkshire Dales

The Pennine hills—the so-called 'backbone of England'—stretch north from Ashbourne in Derbyshire to the valley of the Tyne in Northumberland. The width varies from 15 miles to three times that, but here and there roads cross the hills from east to west, making the most of natural gaps. One such is the Aire Gap, followed by the Leeds and Liverpool Canal, while further north there is Stainmore, followed by the River Greta and the place where the Roman Legions marched across. Between these two natural breaks there is a tumble of wild hill country known as the Yorkshire Dales or simply the Dales.

The Dales were never entirely a Yorkshire affair and more so since the reorganisation of the counties in 1974. Most of the area now falls in North Yorkshire, but it also touches on West Yorkshire, Cumbria, Co. Durham and (whisper it !) Lancashire. In general terms it can be said to extend from Barnard Castle in the north to Ilkley in the south, and from Sedbergh in the west to Richmond in the east. It consists of a series of long valleys or dales (from the Viking word *dal*), separated by high moorland ridges or fells (from *fjeld*). Many local place-names show Norse influence.

In pre-metric days a fell which reached 2,000ft (610m) was reckoned to be a mountain but now 600m (1968ft) is taken as standard, though there is no hard and fast rule. On this score there's about 70 mountains in the Dales and the highest is Whernside (736m, 2415ft) between Chapel-le-Dale and Kingsdale—not to be confused with Great Whernside in Wharfedale, which despite its name is 32m lower!

Whernside is one of the famous Three Peaks, the other two being Pen-y-ghent and Ingleborough, which combine to make a grand long-distance walk, so popular that it is creating erosion problems on the paths. 15,000 people a year attempt the walk and of the 65km of paths in the Three Peaks area, 21km are badly eroded and a further 21km need urgent treatment. Half a million pounds has been earmarked for their repair.

The most popular of all the peaks is Ingleborough (723m, 2372ft), one of the finest mountains in Britain, whose aggressive shape dominates the western half of the region. It is estimated that over 150,000 walkers climb Ingleborough every year—over 400 a day.

Yet outside the Three Peaks area, mountain paths are not nearly as eroded as they are in the Lakes for example, and some fells rarely have visitors. Some are pretty miserable things, it must be confessed; Rogan's Seat is so dire it is almost a collector's piece! (See Walk 10).

Foundation Stones

A first-time visitor to the Dales, even one with little interest in geology, can't escape the impression that this is limestone country: the white crags, the short bright green grass, the rock pavements, seem to be everywhere. And of course, limestone does play a major part in the structure of the Dales, but it is not the entire story. The varied nature of this region cannot simply be put down to one sort of rock.

The major rocks of the district come from the Carboniferous system; sedimentary deposits laid down in ancient seas some 250–330 million years ago. Below them are even older rocks of the Silurian and Pre-Cambrian times (Pre-Cambrian rock outcrops can be seen in the Ingleton gorges, for example, during Walk 17).

The lowest stratum of the Carboniferous is the Great Scar Limestone (known elsewhere as Mountain Limestone). Hundreds of feet thick, it is usually white and bright and forms high crags and long 'scars'. It is riddled with caves and potholes (this is the best caving area in Britain) and exhibits the features associated with them—dry valleys, gorges, sinks and springs. Where ancient glaciers have scraped away the thin top soil the barren surface is laid bare and worn into clints and grikes—ridges and hollows which form the so-called limestone pavement. The best known is on top of Malham Cove (Walk 26) but there are many more examples to be seen during these walks.

On top of the Great Scar Limestone lies the Yoredale Series, named from the river Ure in Wensleydale. It consists of multiple thin layers of limestone, shale and sandstone and since the shale and sandstone wear away quicker than the limestone the effect is to have a series of steep little cliffs interspersed by less steep ground. The effect can be seen on Ingleborough (where the Yoredale series sits clearly on top of the Great Scar Limestone round Souther Scales), but it can also be seen on a less aggressive scale, perhaps, in Wensleydale. Such an arrangement gives rise to many waterfalls.

On top of everything else in this geological layer-cake comes the Millstone Grit; the boggy, peaty, black home of the cotton grass and sphagnum moss. In this layer, and in the Yoredale too, small seams of coal can appear and it is these that gave rise to the pits on Fountains Fell, for example (Walk 22).

A complex series of faults have left bare edges and sharp ridges, but the whole mass of the strata is tilted slightly down to the north-east so that the Great Scar Limestone is most prominent around Settle but has practically vanished in Swaledale. Hot minerals have welled up and filled fissures with lead and zinc ores and in the north the magma from inside the earth has burst forth to give a hard top of basaltic material which forms the crags of Holwick and High Force (Walk 14).

The Lead Miners

Although coal was mined on Fountain Fell (Walk 22) and other places, and copper, iron and zinc ores have been commercially exploited at various times in the Dales, the chief mineral of the area was always lead ore. Evidence of old lead mining can be seen (by those who know what to look for) throughout the area, but are most obvious in the Swaledale–Arkengarthdale area, and the Grassington–Nidderdale area. These are the two great mining *fields* of the Dales and Walks 10, 11 and 29 look at them closely. They are called fields because the mineral veins are closely packed together there and so there is a concentration of mining.

The veins are usually only inches thick and though of great depth may only be a few hundred yards long. On average only 5% of the vein will be lead ore, the rest will be fluorspar, barytes or similar quartz-like minerals known to the old miners as *gangue* which they threw away as spoil or *deads*—some of this has later been reworked for other uses. Not only is the percentage of ore low but it is not evenly spread: some parts of the vein are almost entirely gangue whilst others are rich in galena, the principal ore of lead. The veins, too, vary in width and a rich vein may suddenly close up or 'pinch out'.

Once a vein was identified there were several ways the old miners could get at it, depending on circumstances. One of the earliest was known as *hushing*. This was applied to veins on hillsides, and consisted of diverting a stream to fill up a dam built above the vein, then suddenly letting the water go in a great wave which swept away the top few feet of material. This could be picked over at the bottom of the slope where the water had dumped it, and the exposed vein itself was easier to get at. Sometimes this was done time and again so that some hushes became enormous gullies—there are some fine examples in Gunnerside Gill (Walk 10). Other methods included simply digging a trench along the vein (often called a *rake* when it is worked) or digging shallow bell pits. Deeper mines involved vertical *shafts* or *levels*, driven in horizontally.

Shafts often went below water level and keeping the mine dry was a constant battle. A level would drain everything above it, but below the valley floor pumps had to be used.

Once the ore had been raised it had to be treated and smelted, turned into pigs of lead which could then be carried away to a hungry market. Some have been found dating from Roman times. Remains of smelters can be seen on Walks 10, 11, 26, 29 and 32.

Lead mining tends to be romanticized today but the work was hard, dirty, uncertain and dangerous. Yet many lead miners were fiercely devoted to their craft just as mining speculators were incurable optimists. There were vast fortunes to be won—and lost.

The National Parks
There is a saying that a camel is a horse designed by a committee, and there is something of that about the Yorkshire Dales National Park. It was designated in 1954 and at 680 sq. miles (1761 sq. km.) it is the third largest National Park after the Lakes and Snowdonia, and yet, as an examination of the map will show, it could and should have been very much larger. The fact is the Park was a political creation bearing little relation to what was needed. It was based on the idea that the old North and West Ridings had to have the same amount of Park each, whilst Westmorland was to be excluded. As a result of this petty bureaucracy the whole of Mallerstang, half of the Howgills, Gragareth and upper Nidderdale are excluded from the Park. Twenty years later the county boundaries were redrawn, which made an even bigger nonsense of the whole thing.

Within the area allocated, however, the Park authorities are doing a good job. There are excellent Centres at Aysgarth Falls, Clapham, Grassington, Hawes, Malham and Sedbergh where information and literature are available, and as we have already seen, they are spending a large amount of money on footpath repair. Money is also being allocated to preserve the best of the lead mining remains.

There are six Area Wardens and amongst their other duties they conduct guided walks,, usually fairly short, on certain days. As well as this there are special interest walks—on lead mining, wildlife, geology and the like—by experts working on a voluntary basis. Details of all these services are contained in the annual newspaper *The Visitor* obtainable free from any National Park centre.

Walking In the Dales
Walking in the Dales is rather different from walking in any of the other hill areas of Britain, even other parts of the Pennines. In the Peak District, for example, if you walk in the Dark Peak on Bleaklow or Kinder, you are confined to gritstone on the moors and in the valleys; if you choose the White Peak, you are confined, more or less, to limestone. There are two quite distinct areas. In the Dales, on the other hand, you can start the walk in a limestone valley, cross the Yoredale series and the gritstone and descend again to limestone. This makes for tremendous variety in the walking. An excellent example of this is Walk 30, across the Horse Head pass to Yockenthwaite and Cray and back over Old Cote Moor. The ascent of Ingleborough is another.

The contrast between the harsh moorland tops and the sylvan valleys is most striking. What greater contrast could one have, for example, than between lush, green Dentdale and the windswept summit of Whernside, highest of the Yorkshire peaks? Yet both occur in the same walk (Walk 19).

In my opinion all the best walks contain some element of this mixture, but we mustn't forget that this area is not called the *Dales* without reason—the long, beautiful valleys offer many splendid walks by their river banks. For this, the Wharfe and its tributaries are incomparable, though I must confess to a sneaking affection for the Swale. A long-distance walk called The Dales Way follows Wharfedale and Dentdale throughout the best part of their lengths whilst The Yore Way follows the Ure and Rawthey from York to Kirkby Stephen.

The long, low farmhouses and drystone walls are as common in the Dales as in other northern hill regions and will come as no surprise to the seasoned walker. There are however, many more field barns in the Dales than most other areas because it was the practice to store winter feed near the cattle rather than in one central area. It saved on the haycarting, but it did mean the farmer had to go round the different barns feeding the cattle in turn, often on a cold winter's day with a half gale blowing. Many of the barns which were once substantial affairs, are now abandoned and ruinous. Some have been converted into camping barns for walkers—a sort of English equivalent of the French *gîte d'étape*.

The other unusual feature of the Dales is the number of 'green lanes' or unsurfaced roads, some dating from the times of the Enclosures, others of hoary antiquity, which cross the entire area.

Some really are green and grassy, others are of hard cobbles or chippings. Many are featured in the walks described in this book.

If the green lanes are romantic, some of the farming practices are less so. Never will you see so many poorly maintained gates as in this area (some fall over if you try to open them!) nor will you ever see as much barbed wire outside the Ministry of Defence. One wonders what it is all in aid of—I have even seen barbed wire wrapped around the top bar of a new gate.

Gear for Walking

Many of the valley walks described in this book can be done wearing ordinary trainers, but for anything more ambitious a pair of lightweight walking boots are more comfortable. Some of the fell tops, being peat, are squelchy in all but the driest weather—Buckden Pike is a veritable quagmire, for example. Some walkers like to wear two pairs of socks for comfort but I prefer just one; it is obviously something you have to decide before you buy the boots! Modern lightweight boots, unlike the heavier mountaineering boots, do not need breaking in. Some are made in suede, but if made of leather there is no need for fancy oils to keep them in trim; ordinary wax polish will do just as well.

After foot comfort comes leg comfort and there's no doubt that mountaineering breeches, made in a fine material and not the old fashioned cords or moleskin, give the greatest freedom. They are not absolutely essential, of course, and I frequently wear the lightweight travel slacks made by people like Rohan and Mountain Equipment. These garments are much tougher than they seem.

Ordinary trousers will do, but jeans are to be avoided because they are usually too tight and they offer little protection against the weather. Some walkers prefer shorts but in the fells the weather can be unpredictable and if shorts are worn then a warmer alternative should be carried in the rucksack. A light sweater and some shell rain gear (cagoule and overtrousers) can also go in the sack. Unless you have the correct gear for the fells, bad weather can be more than just an uncomfortable inconvenience. It is essential to maintain a steady body temperature; damp and cold can lead to hypothermia which is a serious medical condition.

These are single-day walks sometimes lasting only two or three hours and we are talking of summer remember, so to carry your gear you just need a small rucksack known appropriately as a 'day-sack'. Besides the clothing already mentioned you need a simple first-aid kit and other 'first-aid' items like toilet paper, matches, a torch and a whistle. The whistle is to summon assistance in emergency—six blasts per minute is the standard emergency call. At night six flashes per minute from the torch means the same thing.

You may wish to carry a pack lunch and a thermos, but in any case some extra food (usually chocolate) should be carried for emergencies. Resist the temptation to gobble it up out of sheer greed along with the sandwiches—you might regret it!

Map and compass—and a knowledge of how to use them–are essential. A Silva-type compass is best because once you have learned how to use it, it becomes a quick and reliable tool. In mist it is possible to become disorientated and choose the wrong path and the compass can help in this. By orientating the map, too, anyone who doesn't know the district can use map and compass to identify the surrounding peaks.

The paths are well signposted in the Dales and all the walks in this book keep to paths. However, they are not always easy to identify on the ground (most Dales paths are not nearly as worn as they are in the Lakes) and because there are many intake walls to negotiate, it becomes absolutely essential to be able to read the OS 1:25,000 map wall by wall. I have found the maps to be absolutely bang on target, even when it seems most unlikely by looking at the land. A good test of this is the route down Bardale, below Wether Fell, Walk 12. Three excellent Outdoor Leisure maps cover most of the area:

Yorkshire Dales Southern Area.
Yorkshire Dales Western Area.
Yorkshire Dales Northern and Central Areas.
Walks outside the areas covered by these maps are usually shown by a 1:50,000 map as being most readily available. Not nearly as good as the larger scale for our purpose, unfortunately.

And finally . . .

It would be churlish to leave this introduction without any mention of the lovely villages and hamlets of the Dales. They are superb, both architecturally and in the matter of comforts. The pubs, with their local ales and wonderful bar meals, are beyond compare.

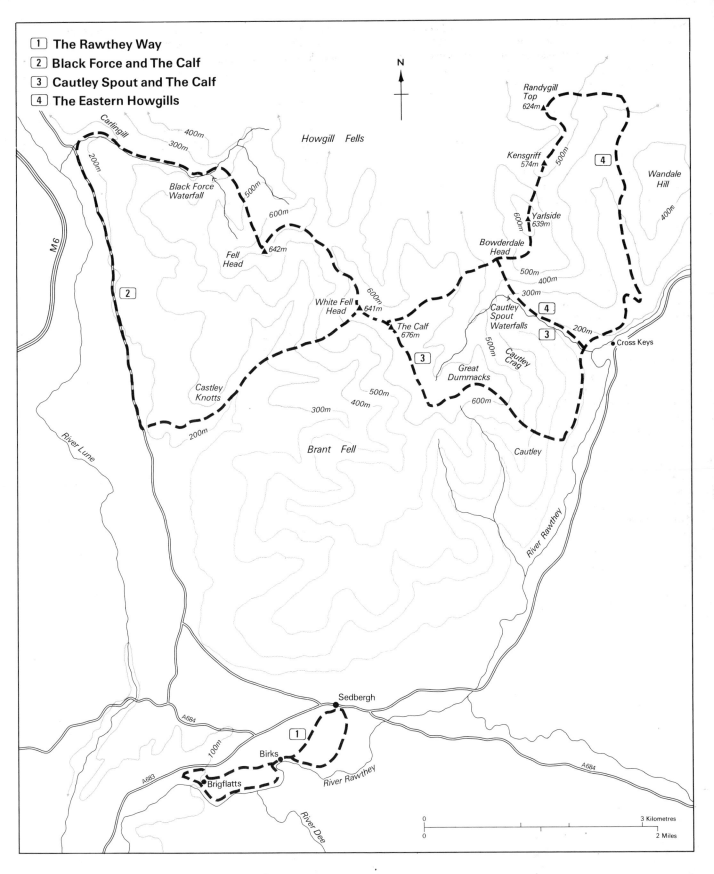

1. The Rawthey Way
2. Black Force and The Calf
3. Cautley Spout and The Calf
4. The Eastern Howgills

N

Carlingill

Howgill Fells

Randygill Top
624m

Black Force Waterfall

Kensgriff
574m

Wandale Hill

400m
300m
500m
600m

M6

Fell Head

642m

White Fell Head
641m

Yarlside
639m

Bowderdale Head

Cautley Spout Waterfalls

The Calf
676m

Cautley Crag

Great Dummacks

Cross Keys

Castley Knotts

Cautley

River Lune

Brant Fell

River Rawthey

Sedbergh

A684

River Rawthey

Birks

A683

Brigflatts

River Dee

A684

0   3 Kilometres
0   2 Miles

WALK 1: The Rawthey Way

Map: OS Sheet SD 69/79 Sedbergh & Baugh Fell, 1:25,000.
Start: At road junction MR660921 in Sedbergh. There are two large car parks at Loftus Hill and Jupp Lane, both within a minute or two of the start.
Distance: 3 miles.
Time: 2 hours, including time in the Meeting House.
What's it Like?: A simple riverside walk for the whole family. Trainers are adequate footwear. Small children need care on the path between Brigflatts and the main road (see text). The views are more pastoral than uplifting, but the Meeting House should not be missed.
Shorter Alternative: Walk to Birks and back using the first and last stages as described. An hour at the most.
Bad Weather Alternative: This walk is suitable for all weathers.

By Sedbergh's River to Brigflatts

The little grey market town of Sedbergh lies in Rawthey Vale, at the foot of the Howgill Fells. It is dominated by Winder (473m, 1552ft), which blocks out any further view of the hills and it is also dominated in a different way by the many buildings and playing fields of the famous Public School. Sedbergh School is of pre-Reformation origin, though most of the buildings date from the last century when the Free Grammar School–'the most prominent school in the North of England'—became a Public School.

On the far side of the playing fields the River Rawthey flows on its way to join the Lune and our walk follows the river to the ancient Quaker Meeting House at Brigflatts.

The Quaker Meeting House at Brigflatts built in 1674 is the second oldest in the country.

Above left: **The Rawthey Way follows this path by the river.**

Above, centre: **The fell called Winder dominates the scene on the Rawthey Way.**

Above right: **The meeting of the Rawthey and the Dee.**

The walk begins near the junction of the two main roads which form Sedbergh's tiny, but necessary, one-way system. Main Street itself is incredibly narrow considering it was once the chief turnpike road between Kendal and Kirkby Stephen, and it has recently been returned to a cobbled surface to make it more attractive. From the junction a narrow lane leads past an estate and some playing fields to a school building and then it continues as a footpath across some meadows to Dent Road. There's a good view up Garsdale at this point and Millthrop Bridge lies a little way down the lane, spanning the Rawthey and carrying the road to Dent.

Just before the bridge a stile on the right gives access to a footpath which crosses a field to some woods, where in spring the scent of wild garlic can be almost overpowering. The route isn't all that obvious at this point but with luck you'll emerge at the top edge of the woods where a path leads towards a ruined stone summer house on a slight eminence above the river. The route then follows the narrow land between the river and the various school playing fields (most of Sedbergh seems occupied by playing fields of one sort or another!) until it reaches Birks House and the delightful hamlet of Birks itself.

At one time the hamlet served the large water-powered cotton mill which lies just beyond, but the mill has long ceased to function as such and the cottages are now of the 'des. res.' type, which would have astonished the original occupants! The short stretch of road to the mill is soon accomplished and at its very end the path by the river begins again. In fact it is now closer to the water than it was before and soon another stream can be seen joining the Rawthey—the River Dee, coming from Dentdale.

Straight ahead lies the long embankment of the old Ingleton–Tebay railway, which last carried passengers in 1953. The lines have gone long since and the bridge across the Rawthey is in a dilapidated condition. There is a path which climbs up the embankment and descends again on the other side to continue the riverside walk past an old mill and wheelhouse, possibly the remains of a small flax or cotton mill according to one authority, though I suspect it was an even earlier corn mill.

The path has now reached Brigflatts, but it by-passes the hamlet, keeping to the river very closely indeed. In fact, there are places where it teeters on the edge of a nasty drop. It is also muddy—the only place on the whole walk where the path is less than very good.

Before long the path emerges onto the main road. Across the fields opposite can be seen the

Sedbergh Church. (Photo: Duncan Unsworth.)

large buildings of Ingmire Hall, a 17th-century house partially destroyed by fire in 1928. This is the turning point of our walk, where we face towards Sedbergh and follow the road for a few hundred yards until a narrow lane leads off right to the hamlet of Brigflatts. It is like stepping back into the 17th century; a huddle of ancient buildings including the famous Quaker Meeting House, built in 1674 and the second oldest in the country.

In those days Brigflatts was a thriving community of flax weavers living in wattle-and-daub cottages which have since disappeared. The farm which can be seen at the end of the lane was in existence then, too, and it was to Richard Robinson at the farm that George Fox appeared in 1652. 'I come from the Lord', he said. Within the next few days he addressed meetings throughout the area, culminating in the mass gathering on Firbank Fell, a couple of miles to the west of Brigflatts, where he addressed a thousand people, using a rock to stand on which is still known as Fox's Pulpit. It was the foundation of a new religion. Fox and his followers had been nicknamed Quakers at Derby a couple of years previous, but it was in the north west that the movement really grew strong and for many years Fox based himself at Swarthmoor Hall near Ulverston in Cumbria.

The meeting place is a simple room, equip-ped with benches and having a narrow gallery at the back. The railings at the foot of the gallery stairs can be arranged to form a small enclosure, or pen, where the worshippers could keep their sheepdogs during the service. In the old days, when the place was crowded, it is said that the smell of sheep was overpowering!

A few yards back up the lane from the Meeting House a gate gives access to a field and though there is no path as such it isn't too difficult to follow the yellow waymarks which someone has kindly supplied to guide the walker to the indistinct and distant stiles. This is especially the case at the railway embankment which once again blocks the way—this time there is a tunnel through.

Up on the left is the large farm of Borrett, once the home of Justice Benson and his wife and the place where Fox held his first meeting.

The way continues stile after stile across the fields until at last it emerges on the road at Birks. This is the way we came earlier, only in the opposite direction, but at Birks House, the paths diverge again and we leave the river to head straight for the town, past running tracks, football fields, tennis courts, cricket nets and goodness knows what other sporting arenas. With all those hearty chaps dashing hither and thither, you are likely to feel quite exhausted by the time you reach the car.

WALK 2: Black Force and The Calf

In Carlin Gill. (Photo: Duncan Unsworth.)

Map: OS sheet SD 69/79 Sedbergh & Baugh Fell, 1:25,000.

Start: MR624996. At the Carlingill bridge, where there is a distinct loop in the road. Limited parking just S of bridge.

Best Access: From M6 Junction 38 go to Tebay roundabout and follow signs to Kendal (A685). The road crosses the railway and motorway and about a mile further on there is a T-junction, with a narrow road leading left *underneath* the motorway and railway. Follow this narrow road to Carlingill.

Distance: 9 miles.

Time: 6 hours.

What's it Like?: This walk is full of excitement from the word go, as it plunges into the mysterious inner recesses of Carlingill. Black Force is a savage rocky gash, full of foreboding when the mists swirl round it. Above the Force the walk leads to the highest part of the Howgills.

Shorter Alternative: From above Black Force follow a narrow fairly level path up Carlin Gill above The Spout to a distinct boulder called the Blakethwaite Stone. Turn west and climb up to Uldale Head (534m, 1747ft). Continue west and descend to the junction of Carlingill and its tributaries (4 miles).

Bad Weather Alternative: Drive to Kendal where there is a multitude of delights.

Carlingill and the Dramatic Black Force

The great gash of Carlingill is the most obvious feature of the Howgills seen by every motorist who uses the M6 motorway between Lancaster and Penrith. The swelling breasts of turf, which are the Howgills' trademark, are interrupted by a deep gully, winding mysteriously into the mountain, its inner recesses hidden

from view. Anyone with half an ounce of adventure in their soul must have wondered what lay beyond the mouth of Carlingill . . . and if too often such places tempt only to disappoint, let me assure you that such is not the case here. Carlingill fulfills all expectations.

It is approached along a narrow road called Howgill Lane which follows the line of the old Roman Road from Ribchester on the Ribble to Low Borrow Bridge. The importance of the Lune Gorge through the ages as a passageway to the north is demonstrated here most effectively—the Roman road, the A685 turnpike road of the 18th century, the railway of the 19th century and the motorway of the 20th century all run parallel within a few hundred yards of one another.

The parking place beyond the gill is just about adequate for a couple of cars. The walk begins from the bridge and goes along the true right bank of the stream, crossing over at a junction where the gill branches right and left. Here the path follows the right-hand branch and it is like turning a corner into another world. The gill has cut deeply into the mountains so that the water now tumbles through a v-cleft where the sides are inordinately steep and the bed so narrow there is scarcely room for the path. Except when the gill is in spate it is easier to cross from side to side to get the best walking conditions. Up

above there are signs of landslip on the steep fell slopes.

After about a mile a steep rocky stream tumbles into the gill from the slopes ahead as the main ravine bends round to the left. The scenery here is quite splendidly wild, with a sense of remoteness which belies all those roads and railways lying just over the hill. You could be a hundred miles from anywhere.

As if to emphasise this, the gill now closes in entirely. The sides become even steeper, the bed even narrower. A group of stunted trees, incongruous in this treeless region, act as sentinals and there is no place for a path. The only way forward is to force a passage through the boulders and fallen branches of the stream itself, fighting the water for each precarious foothold. Fortunately perhaps, it isn't steep and it isn't very long. In a few minutes you burst out of the little canyon into an astonishing scene.

The stream divides. Straight ahead there is a steep rocky bower over the lip of which a waterfall shoots. It is known as The Spout—something of a slight to such a fine waterfall, for if Cautley Spout can have a proper name, why can't this be called Carlin Spout? It would certainly grace any moorland stream; an object of attention and admiration, but alas! The poor old Spout loses out all round for not only does it not have a proper name, but its thunder

Above: **Carlingill penetrates deep into the heart of the Howgills.**

Facing page: **Some scrambling is needed to reach the head of the gill along its rocky bed.**

is stolen by Black Force.

A giant has taken a scimitar and slashed deep at the mountainside. The result is Black Force; a rocky gorge of unbelievable majesty in such humble surroundings. It lies to the right of The Spout, dominating the scene with its very presence. When the cloud is down and mists swirl about the upper reaches of the chasm it looks like something out of a Wagnerian opera. It is then at its finest and though I am against taking electronic devices into the hills, an ascent of Black Force in swirling mist with a pocket tape recorder blasting out the Valkyries would be quite an experience!

On a warm summer's day Black Force loses some of its presence. For rock climbers it becomes an amiable scramble, though others should keep off, because it is not as amiable as all that and the hard bit is right at the top. For some strange reason too, it does not photograph well; people will look at a print and say 'Oh yes. That's Black Force,' just as they say 'Oh yes. That's the Taj Mahal', knowing in both cases that the picture comes nowhere near the real truth of the matter.

On the left of the Force there is a steep buttress of grass which is the only sensible way out of Carlingill at this stage. It is a real cruncher, make no mistake, a typical Howgill slope of short smooth grass and very, very steep. It needs to be taken cautiously, in zig-zags, or you are likely to end at the top gasping like a landed flounder. There are places en route where it is possible to look into the depths of Black Force, watching the water splash from ledge to ledge, or across at the great swirls of rock strata showing how the place was bent and twisted all those centuries ago when the earth was young.

On the left a dry gully forms, not as deep as the Force, of course, but enough to make the buttress into a narrow arête like a miniature version of Hall's Fell on Blencathra. At the top a narrow path runs across the fell towards The Spout, but our way lies straight ahead, following the stream, and climbing seeming endless slopes to Fell Head (642m, 2106ft). The summit is marked by a prominent cairn. The old one-inch Ordnance Survey maps seemed to get this mountain wrong, for they marked the summit as 2045ft, when that height patently refers to the lesser summit just to the west. Nor did the old map mark the heights of all the Howgill summits, so that you would not know that by following our present route we collect two more mountains in addition to Fell Head and The Calf—Busk Howe (632m, 2041ft) and White Fell Head (641m, 2104ft). In Britain a mountain is any summit of 2000ft or more (or 600m) and if collecting them is your ambition, it is easy to extend the trip to include Bram Rigg Top (672m, 2205ft) and Calders (674m, 2211ft) before turning for home. This adds a couple of miles, but six mountains in one day can't be bad!

Of course, the reason it is all so easy is because the Howgills have this remarkably regular profile. The sides may be steep but once on top there's very little up and down along the main ridge and it is the main ridge we are now on. In other parts of the Howgills it can be different—try Walk **4** if you don't believe me!

The ridge circles round the huge bowl made by Chapel Beck in the western edge of the fells above Howgill Lane. The Lune Gorge lies spread out, mapwise, and in the distance are the Lakeland fells. To the east, the Howgills tumble away and further off there is Baugh Fell, Swarth Fell and Wild Boar Fell. Only Man is vile: on a calm day you can hear the motorway roar, faint but unmistakable.

And so to The Calf (676m, 2218ft), the highest summit in the Howgills, a trig block in a pool of peat on a small plateau which always reminds me of a badly kept football pitch. Except for those dedicated souls rushing off to collect Bram Rigg Top and Calders, this is the turning point. It's back now towards White Fell Head along a very prominent track which was a major east-west crossing of these mountains in bygone times. The track leads down the nose of a steep ridge towards Castley Knotts; into the very heart of the great cirque of Chapel Beck. There are steep ridges all round and on a fine summer's evening the westering sun tints them with gold, like shot silk in a Chinese market.

Down, down. How steep these Howgills are! Two becks meet below Castley Knotts and a broad path leads straight to Four Lane Ends on the Howgill Lane. It is more than two miles back to the car and the temptation is to avoid the road for as long as possible by cutting across Brown Moor, heading for Fairmile Gate. Take my tip—forget it! It is both arduous and frustrating.

Above: **Looking down Black Force towards Carlin Gill. The gully is a favourite scramble—but only for experienced rock-climbers. Our route follows the ridge on the right**. (Photo: Duncan Unsworth.)

Facing page: **The dramatic view across the gorge of Black Force.** (Photo: Duncan Unsworth.)

WALK 3: Cautley Spout and The Calf

Map: OS sheet 69/79 Sedbergh & Baugh Fell, 1:25,000.
Start: At the Cross Keys Hotel (MR698969) on the W side of the A683 Sedbergh–Kirkby Stephen road. Limited parking.
Distance: 6 miles, circular.
Time: 3 hours.
What's it Like?: The most popular walk in the Howgills because it combines the famous waterfall of Cautley Spout with the highest summit, The Calf. Fairly steep up to Bowderdale Head, but generally easy. Not a bad weather walk because you won't see anything, which is the whole purpose, and it is easy to stray onto dangerous ground in misty conditions.
Shorter Alternative: Turn back at Bowderdale Head. You will have seen the best of the falls by then. Some care needed on the steep slopes to the col in winter, otherwise quite safe. Round trip of about an hour or so.

Bad Weather Alternative: Go to the pub in Sedbergh and hope the weather clears enough for the river walk (Walk 1) or do the short walk described above (note: the Cross Keys is a temperance hotel.)

A Visit to a Spectacular Waterfall

The ascent of The Calf by way of Cautley Spout is undoubtedly the best known walk in the Howgills, combining as it does the highest point with the district's most spectacular waterfall. It is a fairly short excursion but like most outings in the Howgills, pretty steep in parts.

The Cautley Holme Beck, which flows into the River Rawthey, drains a broad bowl-shaped valley at the head of which lies the Spout and the sombre black line of Cautley

The Calf in winter, with the impressive buttresses of Cautley Crags.

Above left: **Steep slopes lead up to Bowderdale Head**.

Above right: **Cautley Spout and The Calf**.

Crags. It is approached from the Cross Keys by way of a footbridge over the Rawthey, then a path which rounds a shoulder of Yarlside and travels, sometimes boggily, towards the falls.

The view remains constant and open; it is a valley where the goods are instantly on display and there's nothing hidden under the counter. Ahead and to the left are the steep crags which look impressive at any time but especially in winter when snow lines the gullies and makes the rocks look Alpine. It's easy to think that they must be a major climbing ground, but they're not—Cautley Crags are all distant show. Closer inspection reveals them to be a tottering mass of crun.

Cautley Spout, half hidden, heads the valley and above it The Calf rises in a great swelling, like a basin of dough in an oven. The waterfall, which drops in several steep sections, is about 215m (700ft) high in total, though the highest single leap is about 30m (90ft). Seldom does it disappoint. Except in winter, when it freezes into a series of white pillars, the water pours over in considerable volume, cutting a deep gorge for itself in the process.

The path climbs steeply up to a broad col, Bowderdale Head, which separates Cautley from the long sombre valley of Bowderdale, running away north for five miles to the upper Lune. Steep sided, devoid of habitation, no other valley I know recalls so vividly the bleaker sort of Norwegian *dal* than Bowderdale—small wonder the Norsemen took so readily to this land and left their names on it.

One of the main crossings of the Howgills in olden days went along Bowderdale, used by jaggers and their pack horses maybe, or perhaps drovers. The path can still be seen quite distinctly from Bowderdale Head, slanting up the fellside from the valley towards The Calf and a steep scramble up to it leads to easier going; a broad highway to the summit plateau. If you want to see the falls at closer quarters you have to diverge from this path, of course, and care is needed—the stream is swift and it is a long drop!

The summit of The Calf (676m, 2219ft) is a trig block in the middle of a small plateau, which I have already described in the last walk as looking like a deserted football pitch. On a fine day, however, the view extends from the Lakeland fells to the northern Pennines such as Cross Fell, and from Arnside Knott to the Three Peaks.

One feature of these hills is that though they may be steep to ascend, once on top there is very little work of an up and down nature. You can skip from one to the other quite happily without too much effort. (But beware! Walk 4 will come as a nasty shock.) With this in mind it is easy to turn south from The Calf and stroll across to Bram Rigg Top (672m, 2205ft) and

Cautley Spout. (Photo: Duncan Unsworth.)

Calders (674m, 2211ft). At Calders there's a wire fence which guides us east towards another top, Great Dummacks (661m, 2169ft). Since in Britain a mountain is anything over 2000ft (600m) this little lot represents four mountains within a space of twenty minutes or so!

Great Dummacks really is out on a limb, and a rather nasty one too if the weather clamps in and you can't see where you are going, because it ends in Cautley Crags. The only escape is south-east; anything remotely northwards is fraught with danger, for if you miss the crags you'll end up at Cautley Spout instead, funnelled that way by the Red Gill Beck. In clear weather there's no problem: the way lies down the steep slopes of the fell towards the Rawthey valley until a good track is met, running along the fellside, parallel to the river, which leads back to Cautley and the Cross Keys.

WALK 4: The Eastern Howgills

4.1
The Howgills.

Map: The Howgill Fells, 1:40,000. Harvey Map Services. It is not quite all on the OS 1:25000 SD 69/79.
Start: At the Cross Keys Hotel (MR698969) on the W side of the A683 Sedbergh-Kirkby Stephen road. Limited parking.
Distance: 6 miles.
Time: 4 hours.
What's it Like?: An energetic sort of walk with much more up and down than is usual in the Howgills. Very steep slopes. The walk can be extended to include Green Bell (605m, 1985ft) at the beginning (add 45 mins) and can be joined to Walk 10 at Bowderdale Head (add 1½ hours).
Shorter Alternative: From the summit of Yarlside it is possible to descend the steep grass slopes over Ben End direct to the footbridge by the Cross Keys. Much less interesting and doesn't save all that much time.
Bad Weather Alternative: See Walk 12.

Along Westerdale to Randygill Top and Yarlside

Anyone who has walked the Howgill fells soon becomes acquainted with their characteristic features which are very steep slopes, short springy turf (delightful to walk on) and an almost uniform height, which makes the ridges easy excursions. Only in the east does the pattern change and there the peaks are more separate, more individualistic and a greater challenge. Two of them are mountains in as much as they pass the magic 2000-ft mark (600m) and fine peaks they are too, especially Yarlside, which can fairly claim to be the best looking mountain in the Howgills.

So there's quite a bit of up and down involved in this walk—2000 feet of both to be exact—and mostly on very steep slopes without paths.

The walk commences at the Cross Keys on the Sedbergh to Kirkby Stephen road where there's a footbridge over the Rawthey. This is the same start as for the last walk, but this time our path leads in the opposite direction, into the valley of Westerdale. Here Backside Beck joins the Rawthey but the footpath keeps well above the stream until very shortly a descent is made to another footbridge and a path in the field beyond it climbs to the farm at Narthwaite. Between the barns and across the farmyard a bridle path can be found which leads up Westerdale to the abandoned farm at Mountain View.

The ascent of the dale is very gradual and since the walking is easy there is plenty of opportunity to take stock of your surroundings. The path lies on a flank of Wandale Hill and across the valley lies Yarlside, Kensgriff, and Randygill Top. Each looks fearsomely steep and both Yarlside and Kensgriff have places which are steeper still, almost crag-like. In winter the lonely valley and the steep fells present a savage scene—the sort of place you expect to meet wolves or a marauding bear—but in summer the view is softened by the trees in the valley bottom.

At Mountain View a farm gate gives access to the upper valley where a thin track climbs towards a broad saddle between Wandale Hill and Stockless. The river is on the left and now running in a deep ravine which has to be crossed higher up as opportunity presents itself. One of the feeder streams comes down from the col between Randygill Top and Stockless and this is the way we want to go, climbing the slopes as best we can, puffing and panting until at last the col is reached.

But it is worth the effort, for what a splendid saddle this is! The little valley of Weasdale lies below, boggy and barren, whilst a fine grassy ridge runs up to the summit of Randygill Top (624m, 2047ft).

The top turns out to be a little dome-like field with superb views in every direction. Over in the west the high fells of Lakeland stretch in continuous array from the Old Man of Coniston to Blencathra whilst in the other directions are the various Pennine groups from Cross Fell in the north to Wild Boar Fell and Ingleborough, in the east and south. On a clear winter's day, with snow lying, this panorama is particularly breathtaking—but Randygill Top in winter is a lonely place, not without danger.

Yarlside, one of the finest peaks in the Howgills, with Bowderdale Head on its left.

Winter in Westerdale.

The more immediate surroundings are also attractive. The ridges and deep troughs of the Howgills are revealed in their complexity; hump upon hump, like a shoal of stranded whales and most impressive is the long, long, valley of Bowderdale which runs below our mountain like some deep primeval trench. The way ahead can be seen too, with brutal clarity. Kensgriff doesn't look too bad, though the slope down from Randygill Top seems a bit excessive, but Yarlside looks a real cruncher!

Down—and tentatively, for the appearance of the slope does not lie. It really is *very* steep and there is no path—we saw the last of those in Westerdale. It is tiring and you now know how a haggis must feel, trained to run round Scottish mountains with one leg shorter than the other. *(NB. They can only be shot in season—Ed.)* But this is no place to ponder the fate of the haggis, because you need all your wits about you to get down without a tumble. The end comes amazingly quickly; the ground levels out, rises a bit, and before you know it you are across Kensgriff (574m, 1883ft) and

standing below the slopes of Yarlside.

On a hot summer's day the prospect is fairly daunting. The climb is as steep as it looks, comparable with that of Whernside from Greensett Tarn, but it can be alleviated a bit by slanting to the right and striking the ridge rising from Bowderdale. This leads in fine fashion to the summit (639m, 2097ft).

A stream which is the headwater of Bowderdale Beck, cuts into Yarlside just south of the summit and with caution, for the slopes are again steep, it is possible to climb down to the saddle at Bowderdale Head. It is worthwhile doing this because you get the finest of all views of Cautley Spout, the famous waterfall. It looks like a silver ribbon tossed down the mountainside.

From Bowderdale Head it is quite in order to join Walk 12 over The Calf, Bram Rigg Top, Calders and Great Dummacks, thus collecting six mountain tops in one outing. Or you may think the slopes of Yarlside were the last straw and that it is time to walk down the good, swift path, back to the car and the pub.

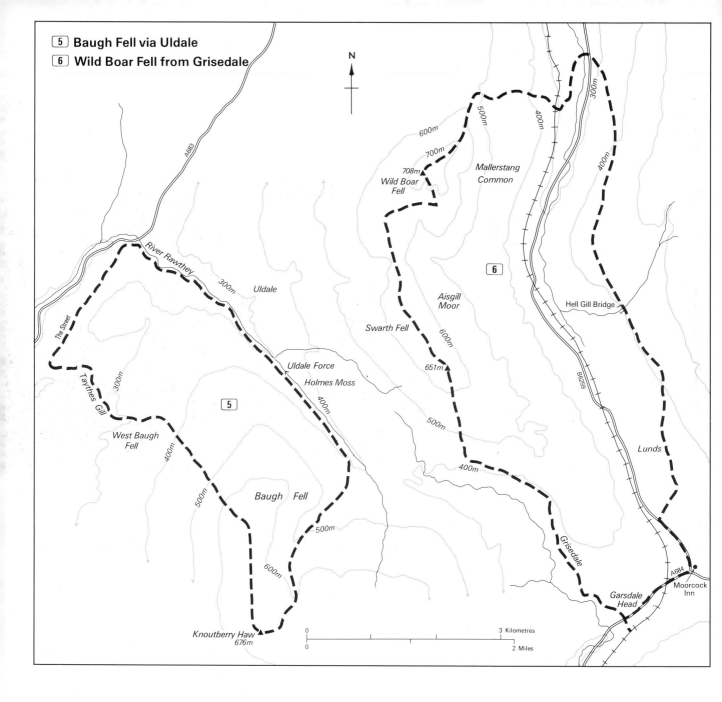

5 **Baugh Fell via Uldale**

6 **Wild Boar Fell from Grisedale**

N

A683

River Rawthey

Uldale

The Street

Taythes Gill

300m

300m

West Baugh Fell

400m

500m

5

Uldale Force

Holmes Moss

400m

Baugh Fell

500m

600m

Knoutberry Haw
676m

0   3 Kilometres

0   2 Miles

600m

700m

708m

Wild Boar Fell

500m

400m

300m

300m

Mallerstang Common

400m

6

Aisgill Moor

Swarth Fell

600m

651m

500m

Hell Gill Bridge

B6259

400m

Lunds

400m

Grisedale

Garsdale Head

Moorcock Inn

A684

WALK 5: Baugh Fell via Uldale

Entering Taythes Gill on the descent of Baugh Fell.

Map: OS sheet 69/79 Sedbergh and Baugh Fell, 1:25,000.
Start: Car-park on N side of A683 near Rawthey Bridge (MR710979).
Distance: 11 miles.
Time: 6 hours.
What's it Like?: A superb beckside walk, one of the best of its kind, with an interesting descent. It is amazing that such an undistinguished fell could hide such a magnificent outing!
Shorter Alternative: It saves 30 mins or more by descending directly to Rawthey Bridge via the knoll called Bluecaster (712969), but you miss Taythes Gill, which is a pity.
Bad Weather Alternative: None. Escape to the pub at Sedbergh or Dent and do one of the shorter river walks if the weather improves.

Following the River Rawthey to its Source

Baugh Fell is one of the trio of peaks between the Howgills and the Mallerstang fells, of which the other two, Swarth Fell and Wild Boar Fell, are much better known. As a summit it has absolutely nothing going for it and it would be a prime contender for the dubious honour of being the most boring hill in the Pennines but for the valleys which surround it and the gills which cut deep into its flanks. It is the sort of place where the journey is everything and the goal nothing. Yet technically at least, it is a mountain. The summit is called Knoutberry Haw and stands 676m (2218ft) above mean sea level, although Tarn Rigg Hill, half a mile east, has lately been elevated to 678m. There is a trig block hiding behind a wall (like the one on High Street in the Lake District) and acres of damn-all stretching to the horizon, for if nothing else, Baugh Fell is at least massive.

Cutting deep into the northern side of this extensive fell is the valley of Uldale, formed by the upper reaches of the Rawthey river, a tributary of the Lune. It is a narrow, secret place where man scarcely treads and the lonely buzzard rises on silent thermals.

The walk begins at the excellent car-park by Rawthey Bridge. A gate gives access to the open moor and to a broad cart track known as The Street which was once the main road between Sedbergh and Kirkby Stephen. The way we want turns off this, however, to follow a lesser path by the stream and almost immediately one is aware that this is no ordinary moorland beck, but a stream of mystery and romance, like a river in Camelot.

The valley is narrow and fairly steep-sided. On the far side small woods cluster, half hiding a couple of ancient dwellings beyond which in the distance the broad outlines of Swarth Fell form a brooding backcloth. The path descends to the river which here trickles over a slabby bed. Then comes the first of the marvellous waterfalls which make this walk so memorable; a small cascade, but perfectly formed like something in a Chinese garden. Further on there are more cascades including a quite startling one tumbling down Whin Stone Gill. When the becks are in spate, all these waterfalls are quite memorable and the noise they make, deafening.

At Rawthey Gill Quarry—a small, hopeless-looking endeavour—you begin to realise that in a curious way the walk is not as easy as it seemed. Nowhere is it possible to stride out. The sides of the valley are too steep, the bed too rocky. Suddenly, this impression is dramatically reinforced. An airy path, little more than a sheep trod, traverses the edge of a nasty little drop and leads onto some extremely steep grass slopes, topped by small cliffs, which form a secret hollow in the hills. At the back of this amphitheatre the stream falls over a sharp broad edge, perhaps twenty feet high, perhaps more—Uldale Force.

In spate it is truly magnificent—a smaller version of Teesdale's High Force—but the steep surroundings can then be tricky and possibly dangerous. The only way out of the hollow is to retreat the way we have come until some very steep grass slopes allow an escape to the upper rim of the valley. Beyond Uldale

Force, the romantic nature of the stream continues as it cuts its way through a small curving gorge called Dockholmes. In dry weather it is possible to keep to the slabby bed until forced to climb out by yet another waterfall, when we find ourselves in a landscape which, unnoticed by us until that moment, has dramatically changed. The romance has gone in a twist of the stream. Instead of the lush gorge there is a raw moorland beck bounded by steep breasts of fellside not unlike those of the neighbouring Howgills. No trees now: just the stones, the water and the remnants of cotton grass.

The beck turns sharp right, climbing steeply. But then the angle eases and there you are, out on the summit plateau, heading towards the wall and the trig block.

Baugh Fell makes an unusual and interesting viewpoint, because you see all the familiar fells from slightly the wrong angle so you can play guessing games over what's what among the tumbling blue contours. Near at hand Wild Boar Fell and Swarth Fell are obvious and so are the Howgills. Pen-y-ghent isn't too difficult to determine in the far distance, but who can sort out the tumbled masses of Whernside, Gragareth and the like?

Curious, too, how the journey back is laid out like a map at your feet. You can actually see all but the last few yards to the car park stretching away before you, like the tilted baize of a billiards table. A few landmarks are prominent: the flash of sunlight on the tarn of West Baugh Fell, some prominent cairns, and

The Street is the old road along Garsdale and leads back to Rawthey Bridge.

in the far distance, a trace of woodland, indicating Taythes Gill. The eye encompasses four miles as if one could stretch out and touch it.

There is no path the way we want to go, nor is one necessary. Through the cotton grass down towards the prominent cairns resting on what from above seems like a plateau but isn't. The cairns mark nothing, as far as I can tell, and the whole area is curiously reminiscent of the South African veldt. A covered wagon wouldn't be out of place.

A little further and the land tips over an edge. Taythes Gill is clearer now. The descent is stepper than it seems from above and entry to the gill is at first impossible because the sides are too sheer, but eventually it is possible to scramble down to the bed of the watercourse where it pours over in a splendid fall. Beyond that, half hidden by trees, the stream plunges into a deep canyon, forcing the walker out of the gill to go teetering along steep grass slopes, wishing he had one leg longer than the other.

Before long a path appears, well above the gill, and this is certainly the recommended route. A friend and I once took advantage of a long dry spell to force our way along the stream bed through tumbled trees, the debris of winter storms. With the gill in spate, this would be impossible or at least very hazardous, but for us the sun glinted off a dry rock bed. Only a trickle of water passed through. Though not without interest, the expedition was exhausting and in the end we had to give up.

An ancient bridge spans the stream, with a track which leads to Taythes Farm, but this is not our way. Instead, we follow another path along the banks of the stream to a perfect miniature col beyond which lies a grassy hollow so lonely it seems a million miles from nowhere. And yet all is illusion, for just over the lip of the hollow, scarcely a hundred yards away, is The Street and the way back to the car.

WALK 6: Wild Boar Fell from Grisedale

Map: Most of the walk is on OS Sheet SD69/ 79, 1:25,000. The missing bit—about half a mile at the start of The High Way—is not vital.
Start: At road junction MR786920. Park off the small road.
Distance: 14¹/₂ miles.
Time: 8 hours.
What's it Like?: A very fine and varied walk. The way off Wild Boar Fell can be problematical if you don't hit the right route because of the railway line, and the first bit of The High Way can be unpleasant in muddy conditions, but otherwise the going is good throughout.
Shorter Alternatives: 1) Park near the top of the narrow road over Wharton Fell (MR769035) (good parking) and follow the ridge over Little Fell to The Nab and Wild Boar Fell, returning the same way (3¹/₂ hours); 2) Various short walks can be made round Lunds incorporating part of The High Way.

Bad Weather Alternatives: Escape to the fleshpots of Hawes, Sedbergh or Kirkby Stephen. The two first named have excellent antiquarian bookshops.

The Lost Valley of Grisedale to Lady Anne's Road

Grisedale is the lost valley of the Dales; a quiet backwater whose very existence is largely unsuspected by the tourists who pass through Garsdale on their way from Sedbergh to Hawes. It is hidden from the road by a swelling of fellside and it is little more than a deep hollow between Baugh Fell on the one hand and Swarth Fell on the other. There's a scattering of ancient dwellings (mostly being done up by offcomers now), a meandering beck and meadows made golden by the marsh

Ais Gill and Wild Boar Fell. (Photo: Duncan Unsworth.)

A lonely farm in Grisedale. (Photo: Duncan Unsworth.)

There is no path to speak of but the natural line seems to take you towards the eastern edge and the tall cairns which are perched on the brim of the plateau with the Mallerstang valley directly below and grim Mallerstang Edge across, looking high and bleak and not at all a friendly place.

The cairns are largely ruinous, neither as tall nor as well made as those on Nine Standards Rigg (see Walk 8), but why anyone should want to build them in the first place is a complete mystery. Several of the peaks in this corner of the Dales exhibit this obsession with tall cairns and one begins to suspect strange rituals at the midsummer solstice. Perhaps Merlin had a hand in it?

The top of the fell is a bit like a big football pitch. The actual summit cairn (a massive affair) lies on the western edge (708m, 2323ft) and from it there are splendid views of the Howgills and Ravenstonedale (which is pronounced Rassendal, believe it or not). By following the edge round to the north you come to a narrow rocky neck of the fell known as The Nab where a path leads down a steep spur to meet a 'crossroads', a major path from Ravenstonedale to Mallerstang. This is our way down into the valley, but in my experience it isn't easy to follow for after an initial promise of a good slanting rake it deposits the walker in a limestone wilderness in which he must find his own salvation. If you are not too frustrated with the route finding at this point it is worth noticing the junction between the limestone and the overlying gritstone. It is this, as much as anything, which gives Wild Boar Fell its distinctive outline.

With a bit of luck, however, you'll find a tunnel under the railway and come out at Hazelgill Farm. There is a right of way across the flat meadows to the next farm north, at Deep Gill, where an ancient bridge crosses the infant River Eden and joins the B6259, Mallerstang road.

Almost directly across the road from the track to Deep Gill there is a gate which gives access to the road made famous by the redoubtable Lady Anne Clifford who in the 17th century used it to visit her castle at Mallerstang, Pendragon. Pendragon is now a sorry ruin, but it was like that once before, after the Scots burnt it in 1541. A century later Anne spent good money putting it in order as she did with all her castles, even though the age of castles was long since past. She was a proud lady; proud of her name and her inheritance—though it must be said the rebuilding was done

marigold in May. It is the nearest thing to a real live Brigadoon you are ever likely to find.

The walk begins at Garsdale Head near the old railway junction where the Galloway Gate road comes down off Garsdale Common. There's good parking here and it only takes a minute to walk back to the main road and cross it to a stile pointing the way to Grisedale and Flust—Flust being the highest dwelling in the dale. There is no path to speak of, but the way is obvious across the swelling of fellside and down into the meadows to join the narrow dale road at Rowantree farm. Baugh Fell, huge and lumpy, rises across the dale.

The road goes steeply uphill to East House, much restored, then contours round to Flust, now abandoned. Up on the right can be seen the prominent cairn on top of Swarth Fell Pike and a direct ascent of the fell is made towards it. It is quite a pull, but then the ascent eases and there is a gradual rise to the summit of Swarth Fell itself (681m, 2234ft). Over in the west there are good views of the Howgills and nearer to hand, across the great mountain hollow carved out of the fells by Ais Gill, lies the edge of Wild Boar Fell. Some of the tall cairns for which the hill is famous can be seen, like stone giants guarding an ancient earthwork and one remembers that this is no ordinary land but Mallerstang, the home of Uther Pendragon, father of King Arthur.

Beyond Swarth Fell the land slopes down to a col on which there is a peaty little tarn then rises steeply to the plateau of Wild Boar Fell.

27

largely to spite Oliver Cromwell, who had dared to damage two of them (Appleby and Brougham).

The real name for Lady Anne's road is The High Way and a more appropriate name would be hard to find for it hugs the flanks of Mallerstang, suspended half way between heaven and earth. For the first mile or so the path climbs steeply and in wet weather is unpleasant because tractors have churned up the surface, helped by that diabolical invention, the trail bike. Higher up, fortunately, the surface is harder and the path also levels out a good deal. There are superb views across Mallerstang to Wild Boar Fell.

At Hell Gill Bridge the High Way crosses a deep and spectacular limestone gorge (though only glimpses can be got from the bridge) and you are standing on the very watershed of northern England. Hell Gill joins the River Eden and flows eventually to the Irish Sea, yet a few feet further on finds the headwaters of the River Ure which flows into the Ouse and eventually the North Sea.

From the bridge the most obvious path leads downhill to Shaw Paddock, but The High Way itself continues to climb gently and continue round to Cotter End in Wensley Dale. But it is easy to leave it and descend through Lunds past its ancient chapel to the surfaced road near the junction and The Moorcock Inn, where you can have a pint and a plate of ham and chips before walking the half mile or so back to the car.

Top: **Pendragon Castle with Wild Boar Fell behind**.

Top, left: **Hell Gill Bridge**.

Above: **Wild Boar Fell**.

WALK 7: Mallerstang Edge

Mallerstang Edge seen from the High Way.

Map: The only suitable map is the old O.S. One Inch Sheet 90, Wensleydale (See text).
Start: MR781043. Good off-road parking by a gate in the fence, which gives access to the fellside.
Distance: 12 miles.
Time: 6 hours.
What's it Like?: A long pull to the first summit, 1½ miles, then an undulating ridge followed by a rapid descent. Choose a period of dry weather for optimum conditions or it can be fairly arduous going. In mist, precise navigation is required otherwise you could end up in Swaledale!
Connecting Walk: It is possible to join Walks 6 and 7 into a circuit of Mallerstang. Instead of descending Wild Boar Fell to Hazelgill, continue along the ridge and descend to Pendragon Castle. Follow Walk 7 until the descent to The High Way and from this descend via Lunds to

the Moorcock and so back to the car. About 20 miles and a very tough day.
Shorter Alternatives: 1) From the ridge it is possible to descend directly to Outhgill or The High Way by picking a suitable gap in the crags. The crags are considerably broken but great care is needed and this is not recommended as a way in bad weather: 2) The easiest way onto the ridge is from Lamps Moss (MR811042), the motor pass from Kirkby Stephen to Swaledale. The ascent to the first summit, High Pike Hill, is only some 400ft! From there the ridge could be followed to Sails and a descent made via Lunds to the Moorcock Inn (8 miles). Of course, this requires some kind person to drop you off at Lamps Moss and pick you up at the Moorcock, and you miss much that is good about the walk.
Bad Weather Alternative: Flee!

A Walk along the Watershed

Across Mallerstang Common from Wild Boar Fell lies a long range of fells edged with broken crags. In the evening the crags glow golden in the westering sun and the place has a magical air about it. It is easy to believe the legend that this was the home of Uther Pendragon, King Arthur's father and that perhaps the Knights are still sleeping in a cave in the hills waiting until England is once more threatened.

Mallerstang is sternly beautiful, but neither the beauty of the place, nor the legend, prevented it from being excluded from the Dales National Park. The limits were taken as being the county boundary with what was then Westmorland, totally ignoring the reality of the situation. So Mallerstang Edge and Wild Boar Fell were left in limbo, unprotected. One consequence of this is the utter absence of signposts or waymarks in the dale, so you cannot tell whether there is a right of way through this farmyard or that intake.

The situation is made worse by the Ordnance Survey, whose excellent Yorkshire Dales series of Outdoor Leisure Maps doesn't cover Mallerstang (not in the Park, you see) and whose Pathfinder Series on the same scale splits it up into goodness knows how many sheets. Even the 1/50,000 series requires three sheets to cover Mallerstang and so we are left with the old Sheet 90, *Wensleydale,* of the One Inch series, as the only map to get Mallerstang on a single sheet!

The start I have chosen for this walk is at Dalefoot, where the river and road come together and there is ample off-road parking. A gate gives access through a wire fence to the open fellside and by following some deep tractor tyre marks round the intake wall it is possible to climb up towards a limestone gully where the rock is of an unusual whiteness. The gully, shallow and easy, makes a good access to the ridge above and reveals some interesting rock formations into the bargain. Soon the top is reached, Great Bell (375m, 1230ft).

You find yourself standing on a low subsidiary ridge. In the mid-distance is a shapely pointed fell with a large cairn on it which seems to be the end of the Mallerstang ridge proper, but a short walk in that direction soon shows you that this is an optical illusion. The shapely fell is Tailbridge Hill, on the other side of the Lamps Moss road, and nothing whatever to do with Mallerstang! The end of the Mallerstang ridge lies more to the right, craggy but fairly undistinguished and seem-

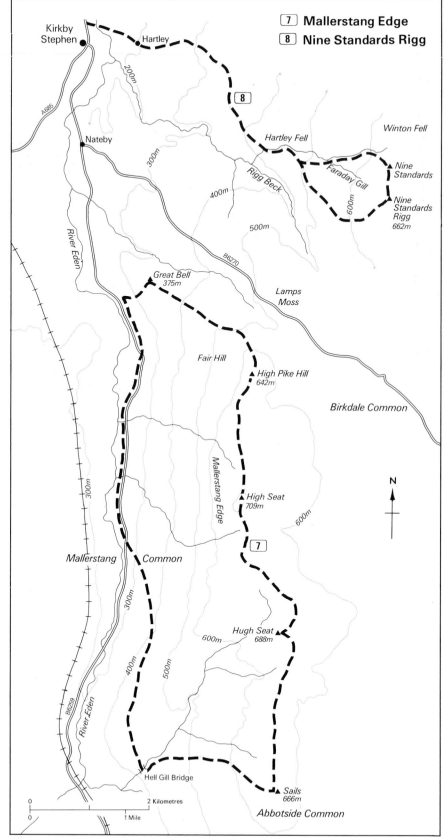

7 Mallerstang Edge
8 Nine Standards Rigg

The time has now come to examine the ridge you are about to embark upon. It is a great belly of a ridge, like an upturned whale and very long. On the left, east, it falls away quite gently in endless groughs (peat channels) and bog. On the right, west, is Mallerstang's dale cut off by crags, though you can't see the dale or the crags from this angle. Two cairned tops show in the distance, obviously Point 2107ft, (643m), un-named on the one-inch map, and High Seat (710m, 2328ft) and it is towards these that we direct our footsteps.

There is no path and the predominant environment seems to be tussock grass enlivened here and there with bog. There are smooth patches, but not many and surprisingly perhaps, in view of the fact that most of the summits are of much the same height, there is more up and down than you might at first expect. After a dry spell the going along the tops is not too bad, but after prolonged rainy weather it can be very boggy.

A series of well-built cairns marks the line of the ridge, not arranged in clusters as they are on Wild Boar Fell across the dale, but individually, sometimes on eminences and sometimes on slopes. No doubt they were all connected in some way with the old border, but now they simply mystify. A curious fact emerges over height—all this ridge is over 2000ft, and so, technically, I suppose it is just one big mountain with a number of tops. From the one-inch map, where the heights are given in feet, there are four named tops, two spot heights and one totally unmarked top which the contours show must be at least 2250ft.

So our route goes from High Pike Hill over spot heights 2107 and 2191 to High Seat (710m, 2328ft). Like an undulating switchback railway it then dips and rises again to the unknown top, then swings round in a magnificent curve to the next summit, Hugh Seat (688m, 2257ft). Two deep gills flank this summit on the west, giving it a distinctively isolated appearance and these gills join lower down to form Hell Gill, the principal source of the River Eden. On the eastern side the streams run down to form the River Swale, so Hugh Seat is a real watershed with rivers running to the Irish Sea and the North Sea.

The unusual name of the peak is derived from Hugh de Morville, who was once Lord of the Manor and infamous as one of the knights who murdered Thomas à Becket at Canterbury in 1170. In earlier times it was sometimes referred to as Hughseat Morvill, making the connection with the knight even clearer. That

ingly very close, though in fact it is a mile away.

Almost from the start of this walk there has been nothing that one could call a path and the situation hardly changes throughout the day. Here and there a half-hearted trace appears, then gives up and leaves you to your own devices. So there is no path on the moorland crossing to the ridge, but at the rocks, which are very broken, there's the remnant of a ramp leading to a well-made sheep fold, standing proud on an eminence like the fort in Beau Geste. There's been a quarry here, too, for the rocks are the sort that cleave into roofing stones at the tap of a hammer.

Gentle slopes now lead upwards and about an hour after leaving the roadside the summit of High Pike Hill (642m, 2105ft) is reached. This is the northernmost summit of the ridge and it has an astonishingly wide view—even better, perhaps, than that from the nearby Nine Standards Rigg (See Walk 8). The 'Nine Stane Hill', as Scott called it, can be distinguished quite clearly with its little black stone men and further over in that direction is Cross Fell, Murton Pike and others of the northern Pennines. Over in the west are the tumbled lines of Lakeland fells and, much nearer, the Howgills and Wild Boar Fell. To the south there's Pen-y-ghent, Ingleborough and Whernside—the last looking particularly good from here. Only in the east does the view disappoint, for tumbled moors, bleak and boring, fall away towards Swaledale.

it was an important boundary point is indicated by the lettering carved into the cairn, bearing the dates 1664 and 1890.

The descent from Hugh Seat is marked by a marching wire fence like the one on Whernside (see Walk 19). It must have cost a small fortune to erect and serves no useful function—in fact it impedes access to the end of the ridge and has to be climbed over.

Over to the east, Great Shunner Fell bulks massively on the skyline and a strong walker might consider adding it to the tally of tops for the day since it stands on a branch of our ridge, but it is an out-and-back excursion which adds five miles to the trip and rather spoils the line.

Ahead, the ridge rises steadily to the final peak for the day, Sails (667m, 2186ft). Again, a number of well-made cairns beckon you on but the actual summit of Sails itself is marked by just a survey ring and a few stones. The view is better from Sails than it has been since High Pike Hill at the other end of the ridge, especially into Wensleydale and across to Great Shunner Fell. You can see too how Sails really is the last summit as the ridge falls away rapidly towards Cotter End and the Moorcock Inn.

We turn back from the summit towards a well-made cairn prominently displayed on the western horizon. Deep bog is sometimes encountered after wet weather, though in dry spells it isn't too bad provided a careful route is chosen, avoiding the obvious places. Streams descend the fellside and two of them, only a few yards apart as they leave the morass, go completely separate ways—one to join Hell Gill and help swell the infant Eden and the other to form the headwaters of the River Ure, which flows to the Humber and the North Sea.

As you descend the steep fellside you become increasingly conscious of the deep fold that is Hell Gill, over on the right. You and it are drawn closer by the lie of the land, but there is nothing to fear from the stream at this point because it is only a rocky beck, curving down the mountain. It isn't until it has almost reached Hell Gill Bridge that it suddenly goes berserk, plunging into a chasm of unfathomable depth and roaring through like a mad thing. Unfortunately, the sight of this is now largely prevented by the thickness of the undergrowth springing from the limestone walls—and it is *not* a good idea to try and get a closer look!

At the bridge you meet The High Way; the ancient road to Mallerstang that Lady Anne Clifford followed in her coach as she drove

from castle to castle round her estates. We've already met The High Way (and Lady Anne) in the last walk but on this occasion we are following it in the opposite direction, northwards, below the crags of Mallerstang Edge. It is a glorious end to the day, especially if the slanting rays of the westering sun give the crags a golden glow. The whole of Mallerstang can sometimes be bathed in an ethereal light, and from The High Way you look down on it. Perhaps a steam train, like a child's Hornby model, hoots it way through Aisgill Summit on the Settle-Carlisle line.

What if the last mile of The High Way is spoiled by tractors and trail bikes, and what if there is a couple of miles of road walking back to the car? It is still a beautiful end to a grand day out.

Mallerstang.

Ure Head – within a few yards of each other the rivers Ure and Eden rise, one flowing to the North Sea and the other to the Irish Sea.

The great gash of Hell Gill.

Looking back along the Edge – in dry weather the walking is easy.

WALK 8: Nine Standards Rigg

Map: OS Landranger series Sheet 91, 1:50,000.
Start: At the Cloisters, Kirkby Stephen, MR775088. Parking in the adjacent Market Square.
Distance: 8 miles.
Time: 4½ hours.
What's it Like?: A typical moorland walk of the easier sort, rising some 1700ft in 4 miles. Good roads/paths for most of the way but for about a mile on the top you are on your own. In mist, accurate use of the compass essential. These uplands are very bleak.
Shorter Alternatives: 1) Nine Standards Rigg can be reached from Lamps Moss, the highest point of the Kirkby Stephen–Keld road, B6270. A path crosses the head of Rigg Beck and climbs up to join the Hartley path below Rollinson Haggs. The tendency is to go too far left initially (ignore sign to Hartley) and find yourself faced with the Rigg Beck gorge. About

2½hrs round trip; 2) From Rowlandson's Bridge follow riverside paths to Stenkrith House and then Wharton Hall (now a farm, but grand with it) and Lammerside Castle (ruin). The return can be varied by Moorend. Excellent river scenery at Stenkrith and good views of Mallerstang later. About 6 miles of gentle walking.
Wet Weather Alternatives: 1) Visit Brough Castle. Impressive ruins, (MR794142); 2) Visit the Tan Hill Inn, highest in England (MR897067).

Mysterious Cairns

There are several mountains in Northern England which sport very fine cairns. There is, for example, the beautifully crafted dry stone pillar on Thornthwaite Crag in the Lake District, which is so tall it can be seen for miles around, and the various groups of cairns which

The Nine Standards from Faraday Gill.

34

Looking across Rigg Beck. The prominent barn mentioned in the text can be seen clearly, centre picture. In the distance are the Northern Pennines.

From the Portico the narrow Stoneshot Lane descends to the River Eden which is crossed by an attractive stone footbridge called Rowlandson's Bridge, beyond which a path leads through the fields to the village of Hartley, scarcely half a mile away.

Hartley is a romantic place of mellow stone cottages and one or two grander houses, straggling down a street which is bordered by a small stream. In days gone by the noble pile of Hartley Castle stood at the southern end of the village but very little exists of the castle now. It was once one of the finest in the north of England, but unfortunately in the early 18th century one of the Musgraves, being something of a vandal, pulled it down so that he could use the materials to build Edenhall, near Penrith. Edenhall itself has suffered the same fate in the course of time . . . Hartley Castle is strictly private and not open to visitors.

A narrow road turns left and climbs steeply up past a huge working quarry which is Hartley's one big environmental drawback. At the top of the rise there is a glimpse of our distant objective, then the road dips to a farm before rising again to a signpost indicating the Nine Standards. The road comes to an end at a gate, about a mile above Hartley. It is perfectly feasible to reach this point by car from Kirkby Stephen, in which case the ascent of the fell is little more that a two-hour round trip—but the Nine Standards are worthy of more than that, surely?

Attractive limestone knolls form the landscape here, with contorted strata showing the earth's primeval forces. The road becomes a broad track to an abandoned stone barn which doesn't seem of much note but which is, in fact, a prominent landmark for miles around. It can be seen quite clearly from the Rigg and Tailbridge Hill, for example. The barn stands on the edge of the broad valley of the Rigg Beck which higher up narrows to a dramatic gorge, clearly seen from the path as you climb up past the barn.

The ascent continues as a broad moorland track which was obviously once a bridlepath used for the coal mines up here. This moor was famous for its coal mines, especially on the east side around Tan Hill where pits were supplying coal to Richmond Castle as early as 1384. While the best coal went for domestic use and use in the lead smelters, the poor stuff went to the many lime-kilns dotted about the countryside.

I doubt whether the coal mines on this side

rise on Wild Boar Fell, half derelict windswept, and admirably suited to the name of the mountain. But there are none which match the subject of this walk. Nine Standards Rigg stands alone both in quantity and quality when it comes to a question of cairns.

The nine great cairns go back in antiquity. Popular legend has it that they were built to frighten off an invading army, on the theory, I suppose, that they would look like defenders when seen from a distance. Not for nothing do the Germans call cairns 'stone men' and there are times when these on Nine Standards Rigg look quite menacing, due to a trick of the light perhaps. A less romantic theory is that they simply mark the old Westmorland–Yorkshire border: but in that case, why nine of them? And they are not exactly on the border anyway. Sir Walter Scott, never one to miss a romantic setting, mentions them in his poem *The Bridal of Triermain:*

Come thou hither, Henry my page,
(Whom I saved from the sack of Hermitage),
When that dark castle, tower and spire,
Rose to the skies a pile of fire,
And redden'd all the Nine-Stane Hill.

Unfortunately, you would need something akin to extra-sensory perception to see Nine Standards Rigg from Hermitage!

The walk starts at the Cloisters in the Market Square of the ancient little town of Kirkby Stephen. The Cloisters form the entrance to the churchyard and resemble a Classical portico, like a Regency bus-shelter, but very attractive. An inscription says it was donated to the town by John Waller in 1810.

of the Rigg amounted to much, the surface debris is very minimal, such as you might get from small bell pits. Much more conspicuous is the deep fissure of Faraday Gill which descends the Rigg, cutting through small, broken edges of limestone and is typical of the larger drainage channels on these moors. The Gill is of some importance to our walk, as we shall discover.

The path runs alongside a wall until it reaches two large shakeholes, where a smaller, less distinct path turns off left and climbs to an area of groughs and old mine traces. The kindly-looking limestone is replaced by the harsher millstone grit and as the path climbs the moor becomes bleak in the extreme.

One hot summer's day I came this way with a friend and it was just about here that we conked out with the heat. I've never known a day like it in the hills—and I've been on mountains which are almost sitting astride the equator. The moors shimmered, the sun blazed and in the end I went down with heatstroke. I shivered and suffered stomach cramps. Finally I dozed off for a few minutes—when I woke up I felt much refreshed and carried on with the walk! It was an extraordinary episode.

On that occasion the moor was bone dry, but such is not usually the case. This part of the moor is known as Rollinson Haggs and you will seldom come across a more disagreeable piece of land. Peat groughs, or hollows, and sphagnum moss bog stretch in a wide moat, guarding the summit of the fell. It is good sound cursing country, where you will curse the mountain as you splash through bog up to your fetlocks, and probably curse anything else to hand, as well.

From Rollinson Haggs a slight rise leads up to the trig block on the summit of Nine Standards Rigg (662m, 2172ft). Suddenly the Standards come into view, a quarter mile away, and they startle in their appearance and size.

The view is incredibly extensive. The mountain stands on the edge of its group; a sort of corner block, surrounded by lesser moors and broad vales. That great gash across the northern Pennines, the Stainmore gap, lies at its very feet, so the eye can travel vast distances unhindered. Mallerstang, Wild Boar Fell and the Howgills fill the southern horizon. Over to the west are the distant Lakeland fells, whilst to the north lies Cross Fell, Mickle Fell and the northern Pennines. In the east are the fells of Yorkshire, the lead mining country round Arkengarthdale, and beyond that the flat

country around Scotch Corner. It sometimes seems that a man might take in the width of England at a glance here.

The Standards themselves are not at the summit but a quarter mile to the north and a little lower. There are nine large cairns in a straight line, a group of four and another of five. They vary in height between ten and twelve feet at a guess and they vary in shape too; plain round, bottle shaped and square. They are not particularly well built, yet they have stood there, facing some of the worst weather in Britain for at least two centuries and probably longer. I think the wonder is not whether they have been well built or not, but that they should have been built at all.

If anything the view is perhaps even wider here than from the summit and nearby, on a subsidiary top, there is a cairn with an orientation table mounted on it.

From the Standards the way down is straightforward. Not far below can be seen a well-built cairn, reached by a trace of path which improves after the cairn. It goes down by the side of Faraday Gill, very direct but not too steeply, until it meets the old mine road again just above the barn. It is a very quick way down, and it would be a quick way up too if recent wet weather made Rollinson Haggs a fearful prospect. The cairn can actually be seen

Rowlandson's Bridge, Kirkby Stephen. This attractive footbridge leads to the Hartley path.

The Nine Standards seen from the summit of the Rigg.

The Nine Standards.

from the path below, but you need sharp eyes, for it just peeks out momentarily between two folds of the gill. Strangely, the path by the gill can hardly be seen from the main path.

But to go up and down by Faraday Gill misses the unique flavour of Nine Standards Rigg: you need to sample Rollinson Haggs, see the old mine workings, and get that first surprise glimpse of the Standards from the summit to fully appreciate this fell.

The descent from the Standards is swift. Even on a hot day it takes barely one and a half hours to reach Kirkby Stephen and the bar of the King's Arms.

WALK 9: Kisdon and the Swale Gorge

Map: Yorkshire Dales Northern Area, 1:25,000.
Start: Muker village MR910978.
Distance: 6 miles.
Time: 3¹/₂ hours.
What's it Like?: A varied outing in which the early moorland views contrast with the later gorge scenes. A steep start. The Kisdon Force path needs care.
Shorter Alternatives: There are several variants on this route, some of which are mentioned in the text. On the outward leg it is quicker to follow the Pennine Way over North Gang Scar and return by the Coal Road, but the *best* shorter route would be to follow the Coal Road from Muker to East Gill and return along the gorge path as described in the feature. Say 2¹/₂ hrs.
Bad Weather Alternatives: Swaledale has little to offer the weather-cladded traveller. There's a folk museum at Reeth, otherwise it is

all the way to the splendid town of Richmond where one should see the superb castle, the delectable little Georgian Theatre and the Green Howards Regimental Museum.

Muker to Keld by the Corpse Road

In the heart of upper Swaledale there is a curious circular fell known as Kisdon (499m, 1637ft). Three villages lie at the foot of this fell—Keld in the north, and Thwaite and Muker to the south west and south east respectively. It isn't difficult to walk from one village to another, either over the fell or round by the valleys, but to circumnavigate Kisdon makes as satisfying an afternoon's stroll as you are ever likely to come across.

The ruins of Crackpot Hall look out over the Kisdon Gorge. (Photo: Martin Collins.)

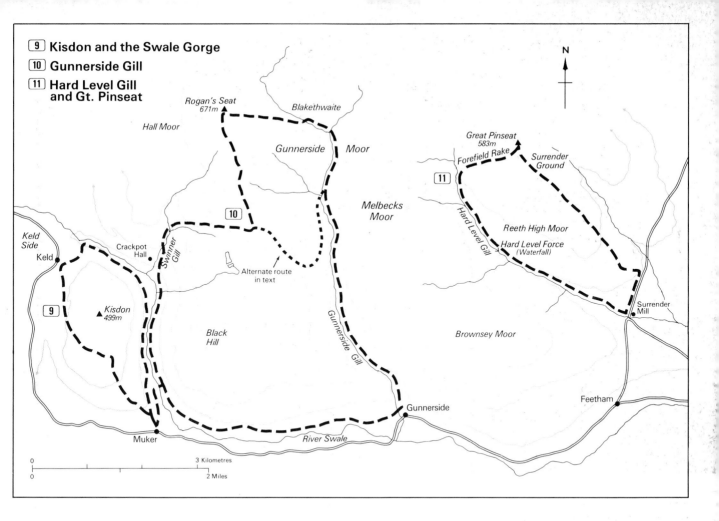

Parking can be a bit of a problem in any of these Swaledale villages, especially on a fine summer Sunday. The walk starts at Muker, where there may be room for the car at the roadside west of the village. It goes up by the Village Institute into the post office square and from there follows a very steep zig-zag lane up the nose of the fell towards Kisdon farm. This road is surfaced, which makes it a bit of a slog, and I can't help thinking it was specially designed for hill-trials in those ancient veteran open-top touring cars that were once all the rage. God forbid anyone should take me up on this—but in any case the road is gated in two or three places, which would certainly inhibit enthusiasts.

Muker falls away below, hunched around its church, looking more like a large castle than a village, so tight-knit are the buildings. At Kisdon farm the lane becomes a gravel track and divides into two at a signpost indicating the Pennine Way, which has come up from

Thwaite and now contours round the fell anti-clockwise to Keld. Our way lies in the opposite direction for a few yards and then, as if remembering its original purpose, the path turns steeply uphill again. It climbs remorselessly until it reaches the plateau-like top of the fell when, all passion spent, it turns tamely to the left and contours effortlessly round the fell towards Keld.

There are extensive views of the wild moors at the head of the dale such as Mallerstang Edge and Great Shunner Fell. Before long the path becomes more defined; a green lane with broken walls reminiscent of some ancient Roman street in the ruins of Jerash or Pompeii and you come to realise that in its day this must have been a road of some consequence. Indeed it was, for it was the Corpse Road whence the bodies of the deceased in the upper valley were carried to the burial ground at Muker. Before 1580 they had to be taken much further down the valley, to Grinton, and the

Corpse Road can be traced all the way to that village. The corpse was carried in a basket on a man's shoulder.

The path soon descends steeply towards the main road which can be discerned in the valley below, leading to Keld, but before the road is reached a gate on the right, tucked away in a corner, gives access to a little-used path which continues round the hillside to the river, avoiding the village. It isn't an easy route to follow; the path vanishes, though the stiles are there if you know where to look—the map is most accurate at this point and should be followed scrupulously, no matter how unlikely it seems.

A gate eventually gives access to the popular path which runs through the woods of the Swale Gorge and this leads steeply down to the footbridge over the river. East Gill joins the Swale here in a most attractive series of cascades, flanked by a grassy bower which is a popular picnic place in summer. From the bridge there is a good view down the gorge with its gaunt white limestone cliffs.

The broad path which climbs up above the falls and the cliff leads back to Muker. The hillside it crosses is the Beldi Hill, once the scene of a prosperous lead mine and smelter and the path itself was part of the Coal Road from the pits at Tan Hill. Coal was carried by packhorse to the smelter and to the villages in the valley. There is a good deal of lead mining remains along this path, not to mention the well-known ruins of Crackpot Hall.

However, the Coal Road is not the best way back to Muker. That lies through the woods on the other side of the gorge and at a much lower level.

In spring wild flowers carpet the woods. The path clings to a steep bank with glimpses of the river coursing over a rocky bed, and the gaunt white cliffs which form the other side. Before long the path splits and a signpost points to Kisdon Force. It descends through the thick woods to below a steep limestone cliff whose corner is fractured in a most dramatic way to form an immense cenotaph of rock which seems about to topple over at any minute.

The roar, however, is not of falling rock, but falling water. Just below the cliff there is a belvedere from which it is possible to get a glimpse of Kisdon Force, a dramatic waterfall. However, the view is not very satisfactory and in order to improve matters, adventurous souls have pushed the path through the gorge, looking for a better viewpoint. This path is home-made, narrow and traverses a very steep

40

Right: **The Swale gorge between Keld and Muker**.

Right: **Kisdon Force in the gorge of the Swale**.

Left: **The River Swale at Keld**.

slope. In wet weather it could be slippery and tricky but it does lead to a place where you can scramble down to the river and get a superb view of the Upper and Lower Kisdon Forces. Those who are not sure footed on steep ground would be advised to go back the way they came and rejoin the main path at the signpost.

It's a nervous few minutes before the unauthorized version joins the main path again, which in comparison seems like the M1. It breaks out of the woods and gives fine views of the river again, not to mention the vast detritus slopes from the old mines, sliding into the river like miniature Wastwater Screes.

At a bend in the river the path descends to the waterside meadows. Over on the other side the deep gash of Swinner Gill opens out, once a prime mining area, and looking like a Beau Geste fort on the edge of all things, high up and magnificent even in dereliction, is Crackpot Hall. What a view there must have been from the windows of that old farmhouse! Racked by mining subsidence and difficult of access, Crackpot Hall was abandoned in 1952.

Along the river bank then, past Ramps Holme footbridge, and so back to Muker.

WALK 10: Gunnerside Gill

Map: Yorkshire Dales Northern Area, 1:25,000.
Start: MR951982—a small car park west of the bridge in Gunnerside village.
Distance: 13 miles including Rogan's Seat by the bridleway (see text).
Time: 7 hours.
What's it Like?: A magnificently varied expedition, full of interest. Wonderful scenery throughout, even in the wasteland that is Rogan's Seat; one of the worst mountains in the world and therefore one which no self-respecting mountaineer can neglect.

If Rogan's Seat is done direct from the Dams (see text) it is very strenuous, and similarly if a direct line is taken to Swinner Gill from there. Otherwise, good paths throughout, with perhaps a bit of extra care needed in Swinner Gill. Not for large and boisterous parties.

Shorter Alternatives: 1) Leave out Rogan's Seat, following the path straight from Blind Gill to Swinner Gill. Saves about an hour, or if you also omit the trip to the dams and back, about an hour and a half; 2) Walk up one side of Gunnerside Gill and down the other—all sorts of similar variations on numerous paths. About 4 hrs.

Bad Weather Alternatives: 1) There is a small but interesting folk museum at Reeth, a few miles down the valley, with mining artefacts; 2) Go to Richmond, a town of infinite delights for the curious traveller.

The Valley of the Lead Mines to Rogan's Seat

One of the chief glories of Swaledale is the number of small side valleys, notably on the north, which penetrate deep into the wild moors. In the 18th and 19th centuries, they were centres of lead mining; an industry which

Rogan's Seat – the summit.

Left: **Looking down a hush in Gunnerside Gill. Hushing was an early way of extracting lead ore.** (Photo: Martin Collins.)

brought prosperity and poverty in equal measure. Lead mining was an eternal gamble, and like gambling it got into the blood.

Mining finished around the turn of the century and the artefacts of the industry—the smelt mills, the adits, the chimneys—are sufficiently ruinous to become almost a part of the landscape. Far from being ugly or incongruous, there is about them an unmistakable dignity of purpose which commands instant respect.

Two of these valleys, Gunnerside Gill and Swinner Gill, form the basis for this walk and not only do they have plenty of industrial archaeology but they are stunningly beautiful in their own right. The scenery in the two gills is as fine as anything described in this book.

And there is Rogan's Seat . . . but more of that anon!

The walk starts in the village of Gunnerside. From the bridge over the beck a bridleway leads along the east bank of the stream. It shortly becomes an attractive path which climbs through woods to the constant accompaniment of the roar of the gill tumbling over its stone-filled bed.

Eventually the path comes out into the open. It passes the first considerable mining remains; the crushing floors and washers for ore. The large bunkers which form such a prominent part of the remains were for separating ore from the different miners. Across the gill can be seen traces of the Sir Francis mine, named after Sir Francis Denys of Draycott Hall in 1869 and the last great level to be driven. New fangled compressed air drills were used for the first time and the compressor tank can still be seen.

The path climbs up the valley side and the scenery becomes increasingly impressive. On the other side a savage-looking gill comes tumbling into Gunnerside in a series of cataracts and waterfalls. This is Botcher Gill—a superb name for such a place, and here too are a few mining remains.

Beyond Botcher Gill the valley narrows and steepens. Tottering crags of rotten-looking rock plunge into the roaring beck so that one is left wondering why they are not swept away by the first flood. Then you think that perhaps they have been, for the sides of the valley look ravaged and torn as if a great claw had scraped deep into them. On our side there are two, maybe more, deep gashes—it is difficult to be precise for all is confusion—and on the other side there is just one enormous gully. These great scars are the *hushes;* a drastic method of revealing lead ore. What happened was this. Where a vein of lead was discovered just below ground on a steep site like the flanks of Gunnerside Gill, a turf dam was built on top, filled with water, then suddenly opened. The rush of water was like a jet from a hosepipe, scouring the surface, removing loose rock, rubbish, and a good bit of ore. The ore could be collected at the bottom of the hush quite easily. It was a method first used by the Romans and it was repeated over and over again on some hushes, like the ones here, which accounts for the depth to which the hillside has been gouged away.

The Bunton Hush, the Friarfold Hush and the Gorton Hush all focus to the very spot where we are standing on the east bank of the gill, though as I mentioned earlier, it is not easy to tell t'other from which. There are remains here, too of the crushing and washing plant for the Bunton Mines.

A little further on and across the valley, at the foot of Blind Gill, can be seen the fine industrial remains of the Blaikethwaite Smelt Mill. One owner is said to have made £120,000 from Blaikethwaite in the last century—a vast fortune in those days, and the Earl of Pomfret gave such an innocently generous lease on the nearby Lownathwaite Mine that when it proved to be a bonanza he died from grief!

Quite apart from the mining relics, the scenery remains beautiful and dramatic, though now the austerity of the high moors starts to make itself felt. The path becomes a ribbon and leads to the foot of Cross Gill where the old Blakethwaite Mine used to be (there's nothing left of it now; the prominent building on the skyline is a shooting cabin) and then through the final rock gill to the broken remains of the Blakethwaite Dams.

When the mines were working the dams held back a head of water to work water wheels down the valley. Now the mill pond is just a reedy bed with the stream winding through it and beyond it nothing but moors of incredible bleakness. Across those moors, exactly one mile distant, lies the summit of Rogan's Seat (672m, 2205ft), the highest summit in these parts, though not the one with the trig block, strange to say—that's the distant cairn you can see from the dams and is more than a hundred metres lower.

The problem is, how to get to Rogan's Seat? The moor is a grouse moor with no right of way so far as I can tell and certainly no path. Crossing it is very, very, hard going over heather, tussock grass and bog. In poor

Left: **Remains of the lead mining industry abound in Gunnerside Gill.**

Left: **Swinner Gill is rocky and adventurous.**

Facing page: **Mine workings at East Grain, Swinner Gill.**

weather you'd be mad to even try unless you are a practising masochist.

The alternative is to go back down Gunnerside Gill to the Blaikethwaite ruins, which can now be examined at close quarters. From there a good path climbs out of Blind Gill and joins a major bridleway which crosses the moor at this point—a well maintained road meant for the four-wheel drive vehicles of shooting parties. Soon the tarn known as Moss Dam comes into view (it used to supply power to the water wheels in Gunnerside and Swinner Gill) and the road forks, with the right-hand branch going all the way to the top of Rogan's Seat.

You might have difficulty in telling exactly when you have reached the top, for it isn't readily apparent. A few stones are piled on top of a peat kop set in an utter wasteland. This is the summit of one of England's most desolate mountains; a real McGonagall of a mountain, so bad it is worth collecting.

The return is back along the road to the junction. The diversion to Rogan's Seat and back costs three miles of walking and pretty boring walking too, but that can't be helped. Places like Rogan's Seat don't come cheap!

From the junction the walk continues across the moor along the bridleway until a sign indicates leaving it for a more pleasant path which plunges unceremoniously down a steep gill leading into a magnificent gorge. Here, on a grassy platform, are some more mining ruins, looking for all the world as though they had been transported from the Inca remains at Machu Picchu. This is Swinner Gill and above the mine, in the gashed crags, there is a cave called Swinner Gill Kirk where dissenters once used to hold their church meetings.

The position you find yourself in, by the old mine, is extremely dramatic. There are crags above and a gorge at your feet. The way out lies across the gill and then down a steep, narrow path which teeters on the edge of the crags and offers exciting views all round. There is a sense of mild adventure about this descent.

But within minutes you are in the valley floor by the River Swale, just where it leaves the Kisdon Gorge. A good path follows the river to Ramps Holme Bridge and then for three miles more, through Ivelet to Gunnerside. It makes a quiet, peaceful end to an exciting day.

WALK 11: Hard Level Gill and Great Pinseat

Map: Yorkshire Dales Northern Area, 1:25,000.
Start: At Surrender Bridge MR989999. Plenty of parking space.
Distance: 6 miles.
Time: 3 hours.
What's it Like?: A simple and safe walk past some interesting mining remains and into some very bleak country. Great Pinseat can be difficult to find because the trig block is hidden behind a wall. The crossing to it from the rake involves some boggy moor and beware old shafts, though they seem safe enough. The return leg of the walk can be boggy.
Shorter Alternative: Walk up the gill to the Old Gang Smelt Mill and return the same way. About an hour. Good walk for kids; they might even learn something.
Bad Weather Alternative: Probably best to escape to Richmond, a town of infinite delights.

A Visit to the Old Gang Mines

In the old days Swaledale was a major lead mining area and the derelict ruins of the industry can be seen in several places. For sheer dramatic beauty Gunnerside Gill (Walk 10) would be hard to beat, but an easier walk is to be found in the next valley to the east, the Old Gang Beck, where there are the remains of two important smelt mills. Smelt mills were necessary to reduce the ore which was mined—galena, lead sulphide—into metallic lead and they were usually sited in strategic places so that the ore did not have to be transported too far across the wild moors, although sometimes this was unavoidable, because the smelter had to serve several mines. Such was the mining activity in Swaledale in the 17th century that

The ruins of the Surrender Smelt Mill built in 1840.

by 1680 seven smelt mills had been built including two in Old Gang Beck—Old Gang itself and the Old Surrender Mill.

The walk begins at Surrender Bridge, where the narrow motor road from Feetham to Arkengarthdale crosses the Old Gang Beck. It is in fact a most romantic hollow, with the road sweeping down to the stone bridge and the ruins of the Surrender Smelt Mill laid out like a Border peel on a patch of bright green grass. It is only a matter of a few minutes to visit the ruins and perhaps observe the line of the great flue which ran up the hillside above. The taller the chimney the greater the draught and the hotter the fire, and one way of getting a 'tall' chimney was to run it as a flue up the hillside. However, the heat of the fire could also cause some of the lead to evaporate and be carried up the flue with the waste gases. Up on the hillside is the Stokoe condenser where it was cooled to metallic lead again, but a good deal cooled in the flue itself and it was the unenviable task of some workers from time to time to crawl along the flue, scraping off the lead. Flues like this were quite common—there's another at the Old Gang.

The Old Surrender Mill was rebuilt about 1840 and it closed down in 1881.

A short distance above Surrender Bridge, on the northern side of the stream, there is a broad track leading up the valley. Formerly a mine road it is now, like so many in Swaledale, used to transport Range Rover convoys of Barbour-clad gunmen to the numerous shooting butts which litter the moors in great profusion. The grouse moors hereabouts are beautifully kept and the butts well made, though I doubt it makes much difference to the birds.

The grouse season begins on August 12th, so you won't see much evidence of the shoots before that date, but any time after that you can see the convoys roll. My wife observed a shoot near Surrender Bridge recently: the birds, she said, 'fell from the sky like rain'.

In autumn the moors are purple with heather, stretching away in the distance, never dramatic, but lonely beyond belief. The bridle-way continues by the side of the stream until it comes to the ruins of the Old Gang Smelt Mill. The chimney still stands, which is unusual, though it is the chimney of the ore roaster, where the galena was pre-cooked, before going into the mill proper. The ruins of the real chimney trail up the hillside, looking like some ancient monastery in Tibet. High above too, can be seen the pillars of the great peat house,

where a year's supply of fuel was stored.

The mill was rebuilt between 1801 and 1807 and it closed in 1885. Ore from the Old Gang Mine was brought here and from 1835–45 there was never less than 1200 tons per annum of lead produced. A few years later new veins added another thousand tons a year to the output.

Beyond the Old Gang Mill the valley becomes the Hard Level Gill, a perpetual reminder of the old mining days, because it was once called Force Level Gill and only changed its name after 1780 or 1785, when miners driving a new level found the going exceedingly tough!

Incongruously, there's an ugly gravel dump with battered machinery a little way along the gill. Do they dig the stuff here or just store it? Large black rubber tyres lie scattered about the site—why is it that people who spoil the countryside are such devoted collectors of old tyres? Pondering such questions brings you to a junction in the track. The left branch goes to Gunnerside by the Old Gang Mines and the great Friarfold Hush, but our route takes the other branch, up Flincher Gill.

The junction is an attractive spot. The stream slides over a rocky bed below Level House Bridge and, as if trapped by the banks of the gill, there's Level House itself; a foursquare stone building which was once a lodging house for miners.

There's a change in the scenery. The steep sides of the gill begin to lie back a little and soon the track turns a corner and enters on a veritable wasteland where it looks as if a giant mole has been at work. If you look back you will see that there's a wide swathe of dereliction stretching to the horizon. This is the line of the Friarfold Rake and the one we are following is similarly called the Forefield Rake—terms which indicate a large vein of lead running across country. The line of a rake is usually easy to follow because of the surface workings—ancient bell pits and the like, where the miners of long ago dug to catch the top edges of the vein.

The path virtually disappears but the way is marked by a series of cairns, the last two of which are substantial affairs, like those which mark the top of some great mountain. Here they just mark spoil heaps! Nevertheless there is a real summit close at hand, Great Pinseat (583m, 1913ft). It takes a bit of finding, though, because one stretch of moor looks much like the next and the trig block is hidden behind a wall!

Level House on
Flincher Gill was once a lodging
house for miners.

The remains of old bell pits litter the moor, their raised rims, better drained than the surrounding bog and lighter in texture, looking like giant quoits. The moor hereabouts is known as Wetshaw and wet it often is. The path beyond the great sheepfold is frequently flooded in places, impossible to follow except by the welly brigade or those who are so wet anyway that they don't care anymore.

There are views towards Arkle Town and the distinctive little peak of Calver Hill as the path descends towards the road to Surrender Bridge. If you want to be naughty here—there's no right of way—a little gully leads off to the right near the bottom of the path and proves to be a very old hush. There's a mine entrance too, blocked with debris.

The road is only a few yards away and it is five minutes' walk to the car.

WALK 12: Wether Fell and Semer Water

Semer Water is the largest
natural lake in the Dales.

Map: Yorkshire Dales Northern Area, 1:25,000.
Start: On the lake shore MR922875. Payment
for parking required. Boating, fishing etc on the
lake are controlled.
Distance: 10 miles.
Time: 4¹/₂ hours.
What's it Like?: Typical moorland walking, not
strenuous and more varied than most walks of
this kind. The outward leg is straightforward, the
homeward leg needs careful map reading.
Shorter Alternatives: a) Reverse the last part
of the walk as described as far as Stalling Busk
ruined church, then follow the signpost uphill to
the hamlet itself. Good views. Walk back along
the road (not far) or the way you came. About
2¹/₂ miles; b) Follow the route described to
Drumaldrace then return along the Cam High
Road to the point at which you joined it. A path
leads straight down the hill to Marsett. Pick up
the route there as described. About 3 hrs.

Bad Weather Alternatives: Escape to Hawes
where there are excellent pubs with super pub
lunches, not to mention a very good second-
hand bookshop!

The Largest Natural Lake in the Dales

South of Bainbridge in Wensleydale lies a
small upland valley called Raydale which
contains Semer Water, the largest natural lake
in the Dales, between eighty and ninety acres in
area. From it flows the River Bain, which joins
the Ure at Bainbridge and because it is only
some two and a half miles in length, is said to
be the shortest river in the country.

Three hamlets occupy this upland dale:
Countersett, Stalling Busk and Marsett, which

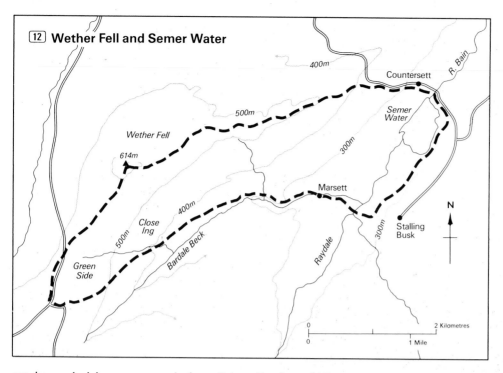

12 Wether Fell and Semer Water

can be reached by narrow roads from Bainbridge or Burtersett. There is no way out, however—high, wild moorland stretches all round the lake, which only the ancient packhorse tracks can penetrate. There is parking on the lake shore at the northern end where sometimes, on a warm summer Sunday, there are people messing about in boats.

Our ambition is made of sterner stuff. Turning our backs on frivolity we leave the car park and march up the road to Burtersett to the point where there is a very sharp right-hand bend and a signpost indicating Wether Fell across the fields. Limestone crags fringe the skyline of the hill and suddenly a great Orc comes menacingly out from the crags, its wings spread like a pterodactyl's. Silently, swiftly, others appear and hover overhead like a scene from *Lord of the Rings*. For once you know how a fieldmouse must feel when the kestrels circle overhead.

The Orcs are hang-gliders and Wether Fell is a favourite launching site for these modern bird-men.

The path climbs fairly steeply at first but when it reaches the plateau-like top of the ridge the going becomes easier. Semer Water lies below, but there is more interest in the ridge itself which rises to the west much more boldly. Experienced walkers will be put in mind of Lakeland's High Street when seen from Thornthwaite Crag.

Before long the path joins the Cam High Road, an old Roman causeway which is one of the most interesting roads of the Dales. It went originally from the Roman fort at Bainbridge to Ingleton and possibly further, to the Roman fort at Overburrow, near Kirkby Lonsdale. From Bainbridge over Wether Fell it is so straight you could almost lay a ruler along it on the map, but at the one point where there is a distinct kink (MR883872) there is a remarkable view back along the road.

We are now nearing the summit of the fell and by sloping up to the right a bit, away from the Cam Road, we soon come to the cairn (614m, 2014ft). For some reason, the summit has its own strange name of Drumaldrace, according to the Ordnance Survey, though most folk just call it Wether Fell. It is said to be the easiest to reach of any mountain summit in England, since it is only just over a mile from the nearest surfaced road and the Cam High Road connects the two places. Doing it this way the climb is a mere 73 metres or about 240ft!

This is the way we go too, from the cairn down to the Cam High Road and along it to the narrow tarmac road which connects Hawes with Buckden across Bardale Head and the Fleet Moss. On a grey day the scenery is less than inspiring; the bulk of Dodd Fell Hill in the foreground and Great Shunner Fell in the distance. Nor does the fact that there is half a mile of road walking help, but don't despair—things can only get better from this point on!

The walk ends along the side of the lake.

unmistakable as always.

With this view in front of you for the next hour or so, there is every encouragement to go forward boldly—but beware! Don't pay too much attention to the landscape and neglect the map, or you'll be in all sorts of difficulties. Nothing dangerous—but if you don't follow the map meticulously, wall by wall, frustration will be your lot. There is no path to speak of and you need to navigate stile to stile. What makes it worse is the broad path which can be seen across the valley and is patently easy to reach . . . stern resolve is needed not to give way to temptation. Trust the map, for despite all appearances it is spot on.

When at last the outskirts of Marsett appears there's a sense of smug satisfaction at a problem well solved, like doing *The Times* crossword over a cup of tea. What a pity Marsett doesn't have a better welcome: it is the scruffiest looking hamlet I've seen in many a long day with old and new farm machinery, plastic bags and rubber tyres dumped all over the place.

A lane leads down by the river and then across the fields towards the hamlet of Stalling Busk which is set up the fellsides a hundred metres or so. Map reading is again at a premium, but without the same challenge as before. The stiles are actually waymarked with yellow paint and so are easier to spot—you don't get that sort of namby-pamby treatment in Bardale, let me tell you!

Still, this is part of the popular walk round Semer Water, so allowances have to be made; and anyway, it's comforting to have your map-reading confirmed now and again.

Stalling Busk remains up on its hill and we pass below it to its old church, now a ruin. It was built in 1722 and the graveyard was used until the Second World War, though a new church had been built nearer the hamlet in 1909.

The path gradually reaches the lake, though without actually touching it. Wether Fell looks fine, but Semer Water itself always seems to me to have an austerity about it which makes one draw back from whole-hearted approval. The legends say there is a village drowned beneath the waters—punishment, it is said, for showing less than Christian feelings towards a wandering beggar. Actually, there were Neolithic lake dwellings in Semer Water so it is easy to see how the legend started. What long racial memories we have, to be sure.

The path reaches the road at Low Blean and it is just a step or two to the car.

Just beyond the junction where the Cam End road turns off the highway there's a gate on the left which gives access into Bardale. The Bardale Beck is the principal feeder of Semer Water and it has carved out a three-mile-long valley as wild as anything you are likely to see in the Dales. The eye sweeps down to the distant lake, with Wether Fell on the left, looking at its best from this angle (well almost—it's better still a bit further down the valley) and the queer lump of Addlebrough (476m, 1562ft) in the middle distance, quite

WALK 13: The Aysgarth Falls

Map: Yorkshire Dales Central Area, 1:25,000.
Start: MR012888. National Park Information Centre and Car Park.
Distance: 3¹/₂ miles.
Time: 2 hours, plus time for pottering at the Falls etc.
What's it Like?: Magnificent waterfalls, especially when the river is in spate. The walking is very easy, well suited to families. Grannies will perhaps find it not taxing enough.
Shorter Alternative: Just visit the falls—an easy hour.
Bad Weather Alternatives: The Falls can be visited in any weather, but a visit to the Carriage Museum and the church will occupy an hour or so. There are two splendid castles nearby worth visiting, at Castle Bolton and Middleham.

A Stroll by the River Ure

Of all the many waterfalls in the Dales those at Aysgarth in Wensleydale are amongst the best known because of their sheer size. These falls are the Niagaras of the Dales and there are three of them, known as the Upper, Middle and Lower Falls.

To combine the Falls into any sort of meaningful walk is simply not possible—and yet all is not lost; what follows is a poky sort of route, but there is more to it than just gawping at the Falls from the bridge. It combines in its short length the best of the scenery round Aysgarth.

The walk starts in the splendid car park of the National Park, which is on the north side of Yore Bridge, on the road to Caperby. From the car park entrance a protected pathway

Aysgarth Upper Falls.

leads back towards the bridge until it is possible to cross the road and enter Freeholder's Wood at a sign indicating the Lower and Middle Falls. As you enter the wood the incessant rumbling of the falls can be heard; there's a sense of latent power screened by the trees from inquisitive gaze and you go forward half expectantly, half fearfully. The power sounds ominously *near*.

This first part of the walk is well signposted and on admirably remade paths which contrast sharply with the muddy tracks of a few years ago. If it smacks of regimentation (and it does—one would not want this sort of thing everywhere) at least it keeps unobtrusive control over the crowds of tourists who come to see the Falls and who were rapidly trampling the original routes to death.

By following the path to its end you come to a rock chimney which leads down onto the flat rocks by the side of the river from where a good view of the Lower Falls can be obtained.

These limestone beds can be followed upstream and downstream by those who want different aspects of the falls, but there is no way back onto the path except the way you came. The Falls themselves are not high, but the sheer volume pouring over, and the immense power of the river are impressive.

Back on the path there is a slight variation for the return, offering another view of the Lower Falls and then a set of steps leads to a viewpoint for the Middle Falls, perhaps the least impressive of the three. On the way back there is a glimpse through the trees of Yore Bridge and the old mill.

A gate gives access to the bridge and our route crosses it and passes in front of the mill (now the Yorkshire Museum of Carriages) to climb up some steps towards the parish church. Though this latter is a mainly 19th-century restoration it does contain a magnificent painted rood screen acquired from Jervaux at the time of the Dissolution, which is well worth seeing. At one time Aysgarth was the largest parish in England—over 81,000 acres!

From a stile in a corner of the churchyard a path leads over a meadow and into a wood, then continues by the riverside, more or less, for about a mile to Hestholme Bridge. The views of the river are surprisingly muted and access to the actual bank is forbidden, but the path leads through remarkable drumlin country where ancient glaciers have piled up mounds of debris, now grass covered. It looks like a mad golf course, or the work of a giant race of moles.

The riverside path can be followed downstream all the way to Middleham, or abandoned at West Witton or Wensley en route, by those who are anxious for a longer walk. It is about 8 miles in all to Middleham through pleasant enough scenery, though not to compare with similar walking in Wharfedale or by the Swale. For our purpose we turn back at Hestholme Bridge, walking a couple of hundred yards along the A684, before a path leads off through the fields by the side of the Bishopdale Beck.

Soon the junction with the Walden Beck is reached but our route wanders through cow pastures by the tree-hung stream of Bishopdale. In the background is shapely Penhill Beacon and the swelling moors of Hazely and Harland.

The track disappears in a caravan site where the temptation is to follow one of the specially created roads, all leading to the exit. There is always a feeling of guilt about walking through

The Lower Falls at Aysgarth.

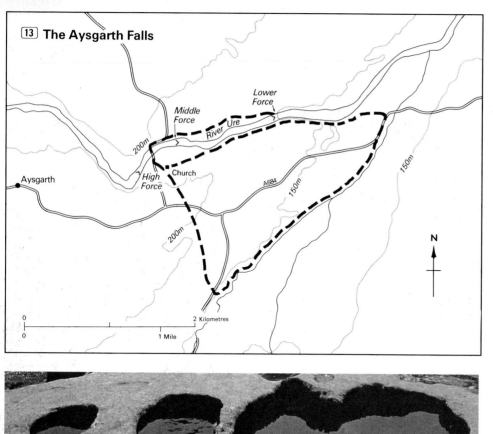

13 The Aysgarth Falls

Left: **Rock pools in the limestone at Aysgarth.**

Below: **Aysgarth Middle Falls.**

one of these places, like trespassing on private grief, and this may reinforce the tendency to escape, but it should be resisted. For one thing, you have every right to be there, and for another, though the original path might have gone, the stiles are all there and by following the beck to the far edge of the site, despite all appearances to the contrary, the path re-appears. A minute or two later the path meets the road at Eshington Bridge and we cross the road to find a stile leading into the well-named Brant Lea, which means 'steep field'. A series of stiles follows, though there is no path to speak of, and a close scrutiny of the map is required to hit off the right place in the complex series of walls. But it is all good fun and the steep little walk is a delight, with some grand views looking back towards Bishopdale.

Before long the path reaches the A684 from where a minor lane leads back to the church and down the steps to the mill. The mill is of 16th-century foundation though it was burnt down and rebuilt in the last century. It was from this mill on the banks of the Ure, that the famous Red Shirts of Garibaldi's army came during the great patriot's unification of Italy. The mill later turned to the making of flour until it closed in 1968 and became a museum.

From the Yore Bridge the Upper Falls can be seen to advantage, but by crossing the bridge and following a path up to the left a nearer view can be got. Though perhaps not as impressive as the Lower Falls, the Upper Falls are probably the prettiest of the three. Here the sills of limestone are at various levels, leading to shoots and cascades of infinite variety.

Back at the bridge a signposted path leads to the car park.

54

WALK 14: High Force from Holwick

A dour winter's day on the Tees with Low Force.

Map: OS 1:50,000 Sheet 92 Barnard Castle.
Start: From Holwick, at the road junction, MR904270.
Distance: 4 miles. Circular.
Time: 2 hours.
What's it Like?: The Tees, from Cauldron Snout down to Middleton is an interesting river and part of the Pennine Way long distance footpath. This short walk chooses the highlights and combines the river with a short taste of the wild moors—of which there are none wilder. The walking is easy though the footpath is in a bad way along the river and is supported by duck-boarding like the trenches of the Somme. The moorland crossing is boggy, but damp rather than deep. If you are a botanist, choose spring for this walk.
Shorter Alternative: From the High Force Hotel it is only a matter of minutes (and a small charge) to descend a path on the N side of the

river to a vantage point from which the waterfall can be seen.
Bad Weather Alternative: High Force *should* be seen in wet weather, to catch it at its best! The shorter alternative makes this easy (see above). Alternatively, drive the few miles to Barnard Castle; a fascinating town of interesting buildings. See in particular the Castle and the incredible Bowes Museum (MR056163) which looks like a French chateau.

Wild Moorland and Dramatic River Scenery

The River Tees comes tumbling down Cauldron Snout from the Cow Green Reservoir, sweeps round Cronkley Scar, then enters upon one of the most dramatic stretches of river scenery in England. The upper Tees gurgles and splashes its way over the rocks of the Whin Sill—curious columnar basalt of a dull battleship grey—with increasing momentum, until it pours with uncontrolled violence over the 70-ft cliff of High Force. When the river is in spate the roar is tremendous, for this is Britain's little Niagara; the largest waterfall in the country.

The tiny hamlet of Holwick is on the south bank of the river, near the end of a narrow *No Through Road*. There's a decent parking spot just through the hamlet, where the road turns sharp right and a bridle way goes straight ahead past a cottage towards the impressive crags of Holwick Scars. This was the original road continued—once an important drove road coming down from the Scottish border to Richmond. It is the way we shall return, but for now we follow the surfaced road downhill until it turns left into open fields towards Holwick Lodge.

At this point there is a fingerpost pointing down towards the river which is discernible as a distinct line of trees. At first there is no path to speak of, but after a while something of the sort appears and descends through fields alive with bluebells in the season to Wynch Bridge.

Wynch Bridge is a narrow footbridge suspended across a wooded gorge of the river. It was first built by lead miners in 1704 and is perhaps the oldest suspension bridge in the country. The miners who needed to get from Holwick where they lived, to the mines on the other bank of the river, must have followed the path we have just come down. The original bridge was by all accounts a pretty hair-raising experience: 'a restless gangway to which few strangers dare trust themselves' as one writer put it at the time. There was only one handrail—and the bridge hung twenty feet over the narrow gorge through which the Tees foamed. In 1820 the bridge collapsed as nine men were crossing it and it is remarkable that only one lost his life. The present bridge dates from 1830.

Unlike the miners we don't cross the bridge but continue instead on the same bank until within a few yards we come to Low Force, a splendid waterfall of two broad spouts, side by side, divided by a rocky islet. At the foot of the falls is a deep inviting pool where canoeists can recover after shooting the falls.

The path now leads by the riverside for some distance. There are rocks and small cascades and on the riverbank a multitude of wild flowers in spring and early summer. Here can be seen the shy violet, orchids, trollius, primula farinosa and marsh marigold.

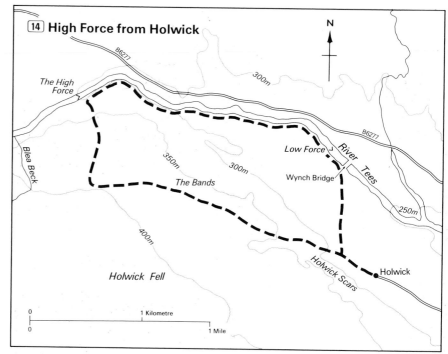

At Holwick Head the path goes away from the river to climb a steep rise where the worn path has been given crude wooden steps which look ugly and are quite useless for their purpose. At the top a gate and sign mark the boundary of Teesdale Nature Reserve, one of the largest in the country. The path plunges through juniper thickets and is now so worn and boggy that it is provided with duck-boards to prevent further erosion. Meanwhile, the sound of High Force has become increasingly insistent; something between a boom and a roar, telling of mighty power.

High Force, one of the most impressive waterfalls in Britain.

Top: **Holwick Scar where the walk starts and ends.**

Above: **The gorge of the Tees below High Force.**

so—voluminous. It isn't the highest fall by any means, but for sheer volume there's nothing to beat it in Britain.

When the river rises a secondary fall appears on the right beyond the rocky islet and in times of flood, the river pours over from bank to bank in one stupendous raging, crashing torrent. At such times it is a fearful sight and accompanied, so it would seem, by all the hammers of hell.

So far the route has followed a good if careworn path all the way along the river, but now for a short time the way lies over open moorland with no path at all. It can be boggy and a bit rough, but it lasts for no more than a half mile or so and is not particularly strenuous. The only real alternative is to go back the way you came, and that seems a pity.

Beyond the Nature Reserve fence at High Force the route climbs gently up the hillside on the left. Over the first crest another hill is revealed, this time higher and steeper, consisting of two peaks with a distinct saddle between them. It looks formidable but in fact it turns out to be short, not too sharp and the edge of a desolate moorland plateau which seems to stretch away to infinity. An incongruous notice board can be seen in the distance and by walking in that general direction you come to a bridleway which is easily the best path you've seen all day.

The bridleway leads across the moors in the direction of Holwick, but just before the village it becomes a private road and the footpath leaves it on the right to pass through a small glen which is walled by the impressive rocks of Holwick Scars. This is the Whin Sill again; the columnar basalt which fractures into sharp edges and straight, smooth cracks. The path is a real delight, but alas, all too brief—in a few minutes it leads back to the car.

It is possible to leave the path at various places to view the waterfall and its gorge. Care is required near the edge for it is completely unprotected and can be slippery, but the views of the fall are quite breathtaking. It is

WALK 15: Barnard Castle and the River Tees

Abbey (by car). The large discount book store in Thorngate is worth a browse around and is open Sundays.

A Walk by Scott's Rokeby

Barnard Castle is the capital of Teesdale; a romantic sort of place, perched above the swift flowing River Tees and dominated by the fortress which gives it its name. Locally, the town is simply called Barney. Handsome 18th-century houses line the streets and some older ones too, such as Blagroves, a 16th-century house on The Bank, where Cromwell is said to have stayed. At the eastern edge of the town, along Newgate, is the remarkable Bowes Museum, often called the 'V & A of the North'; an immense French-style chateau filled with treasures.

The River Tees near Barnard Castle.

The town has some notable literary connections too. Charles Dickens came here in 1838 to write his novel *Nicholas Nickleby,* and Dotheboys Hall is said to be based on a notorious boys' school at nearby Bowes. Here too at the Market Cross was the clockseller Thomas Humphreys which gave Dickens the idea for a magazine called *Master Humphrey's Clock,* which was to contain some of his best-loved stories.

Sir Walter Scott also visited Barnard Castle where his imagination was stimulated by the castle and the fortified manor houses of Rokeby and Mortham. This resulted in his long poem *Rokeby,* a tale of greed and lust set at the end of the Civil War.

So there is much to see in the town itself and it is not a bad idea to do this walk in the morning, have lunch in one of the several fine pubs, then spend the afternoon exploring the castle and the Bowes Museum.

There is excellent parking in the town, either in the municipal car park or in the wide streets of Galgate or Market Place. From there it is an interesting stroll past the Market Cross, sometimes called the Buttercross, then steeply down The Bank and Thorngate to the footbridge over the river. Thorngate Mill now

houses a book store and the other old mills have been converted into desirable residences, but this was once the ancient working heart of the town.

Until the reorganisation of our old counties the bridge across the Tees would have taken you from Durham into Yorkshire, but now the boundary is further south.

From the bridge a surfaced path leads along the river bank with a good view of a cascade which stretches across the broad stream in a long diagonal shelf. The river just drops three or four feet and the water pours over in an endless roar. Before long the path leads into a caravan park but this can be avoided by cutting uphill to meet a minor road, where there is a stile, waymarked in yellow, which points the way.

A tenuous path crosses the fields and overlooks the caravan park and the river, whilst in the distance the huge incongruous bulk of the Bowes Museum dominates the skyline. The path rejoins the road at Egglestone Abbey, whose gaunt remains stand on a steep rise above the road, looking strangely forbidding. Perhaps it is the wire fence which guards the place like a prison camp, and whose purpose is baffling, since Egglestone Abbey is open to the public and free. Egglestone belonged to the White Canons and was the smallest and poorest of their houses; at one stage it was almost relegated to the second division by being demoted into a priory, but it clung onto its status until the Dissolution. Part of the ruins were then made into a family house, which is itself now ruined and makes the most interesting part of the relics.

The road below the Abbey leads to Abbey Bridge, a superb single-arched bridge over the river. Though well hidden by trees in summer, some idea can be got of the immensely tall arch spanning the limestone ravine through which the Tees now flows. It was built in 1773 and the parapet is 76ft (23m) above the water. From the bridge itself there are dramatic views of the river on its turbulent course.

Thus far the walk has been a simple stroll and by crossing Abbey Bridge a path can be found which will take you back along the other bank to Barney, but our walk goes further and as it does so it changes character. It follows the merest of paths, overgrown with dense vegetation, teetering along the brink of the river gorge. A good stout stick is an asset here, to push aside the rank growth, if only to ensure that your foot is landing on something substantial and not thin air! Perhaps I exagger-

Below, left: **The Abbey Bridge over the Tees at Egglestone. Built in 1773, the bridge's parapet is 76ft (23m) above the river.**

Below, right: **The Rivers Greta and Tees at watersmeet near Rokeby Park.**

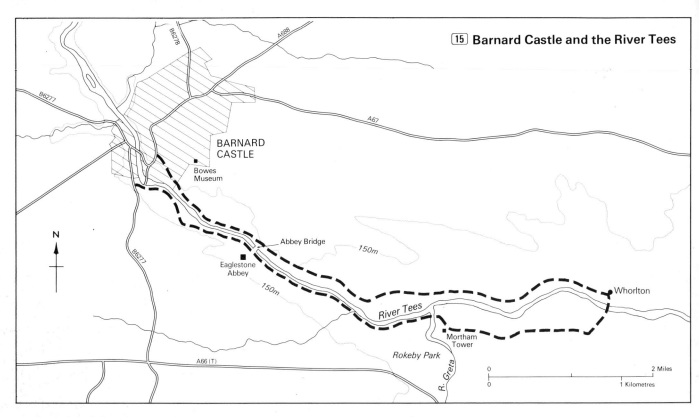

ate the danger—there isn't any danger really—but it is not a place in which to be careless, and the weeds really are head high in places. The trees are dense too, so that the river is glanced only intermittently. It is the sort of place which might be better walked on a crisp winter's day.

This jungle-bashing continues until the path dips into the Manyfold Beck after which it's more out in the open and leads very shortly onto the road again at the junction with a private lane. In this instance (and it is often the case) the private lane is also a public footpath, so there's rapid walking past the walls of Rokeby, with only the merest glimpse of the house. It was here that Sir Walter Scott came to stay with his friend John Bacon Morritt and was so charmed by the scenery that he wrote *Rokeby,* a poem which was so successful in its day that people came in hundreds to see the scenes he described.

Among the places which particularly inspired Scott was the junction of the River Greta with the Tees; a place of rocks, trees and water placed in the most romantic of settings. An old single arch bridge over the Greta, Dairy Bridge, further lends the scene romance and then, to cap it all, just across the bridge and beyond the rise is Mortham Tower, a castellated manor house which plays an important part in *Rokeby*. Indeed, almost every part of

our walk can be identified in Scott's poem.

From Mortham Tower the way lies across the fields past the ruins of West Thorpe to Whorlton Bridge, a creaking suspension bridge that cars are urged to take one at a time. Just before the bridge, on the 'Yorkshire' side, is Whorlton Lido, whose name is as baffling as its function in rain-swept Teesdale! Few places are less like Venice.

Beyond the bridge a long flight of steps cuts out the big bend of the road where it snakes up a steep hill into the village of Whorlton. There's a pub here and it might be time for refreshment before embarking on the homeward leg, but for those who wish to turn round straight away, there is no need to visit the village because the homeward path starts just a few yards from the top of the steps. It begins with a sensational view of the river far below, but then it plunges into thick undergrowth, at least for a while.

But on the whole, the journey back is simpler than the outward leg. The path keeps away from the river bank for most of the walk and even avoids Abbey Bridge, meeting the main road at a farm a few hundred yards beyond it. From there a path sweeps down to the river for the last mile or so, past the sewage farm (no smells!) to emerge as a narrow alley in Thorngate.

WALK 16: Gragareth

Whernside seen from the Turbary Road. (Photo: Duncan Unsworth.)

Map: The Yorkshire Dales Western Area, 1:25,000.
Start: At a ladder stile marked Turbary Road, a few yards from the junction of the Kingsdale road with the green lane to Twistleton Scar End, MR691759.
Distance: 6 miles.
Time: 3 hours.
What's it Like?: The lower part of the walk is through some very fine limestone scars, and there's interest, too, in the Marble Steps Pot, but otherwise dogged determination is called for—the ascent is 369m or about 1200ft. Very little bog—one of the driest of all the ascents described where millstone grit moors are involved. Wonderful view from the top.
Shorter Alternative: Climb up to the Turbary Road as described then follow it north-east to just before Shout Scar, descending by the wall to a gate on the road at MR704784. A famous

road, passing many pot-holes. Walk back along the Kingsdale road, (4 miles).
Bad Weather Alternatives: Ingleton is quite close, with White Scar Cave (show cave) but it is also worth visiting Kirkby Lonsdale, a delightful old world town on the Lune.

The Highest Summit in Lancashire

Until the boundary changes of 1974 which altered our traditional English counties, the highest summit in Lancashire was Coniston Old Man in the Lake District. But in 1974 Lancashire-beyond-the-Sands, as it was called, was transferred to the new county of Cumbria and the Old Man went with it. The new county top was a little-known mountain called Gragareth, on the western edge of the Dales.

Kingsdale and Whernside.

Ingleborough from Gragareth. On the right can be seen the Turbary Road and the copse in the middle distance hides the Marble Steps pothole.

By some ancient accident a thin wedge of land belonging to Lancashire county pokes northward, separating Kirkby Lonsdale (Cumbria) from Ingleton (Yorkshire). It is wild fell country, containing some of the best pot-holes in the Pennines and with a ridge which culminates in Great Coum (687m, 2254ft)—but the summit of Great Coum is half a mile over the boundary into Cumbria! Gragareth itself escapes the clutches of Yorkshire by a mere tenth of a mile. So Lancashire has to be grateful for small mercies in more ways than one, when comparing Gragareth's 627m with the Old Man's 803m.

The difference is not only one of height, however, because the Old Man is one of the most popular and accessible of mountains whilst Gragareth is neither. This is a pity because it offers a classic ascent to one of the finest viewpoints in the north of England, except that there are no rights of way. I don't known what your feelings are in such matters but my own are that it cannot be right to bar access to the summit of one of our major counties.

It is even more frustrating to discover that the ascent begins as a right of way, continues over well-made stiles and then comes to an abrupt halt in the middle of nowhere. Within less than half a mile of your objective you must either climb a wall or turn back! This is the only occasion in this book where such a beyond the stile there are yet more limestone bands. Away to the left is a great limestone block known as the Cheese Press Stone, which has actually been carried down from the head of the valley during the ice age and dumped where it now rests as the ice melted. Further on there is a cairn on a limestone knoll, and since the path has disappeared (it is further to the right) it is a good idea to make towards it and get a good view of North End Scar; attractive little cliffs.

You are now traversing an area of rocky knolls and hollows and the trick is to keep walking in a north-westerly direction until suddenly a bridleway appears, crossing your path. This is the famous Turbary Road; a centuries-old highway used by the peat cutters of Masongill to cross the limestone scars and reach the thick beds of peat in the acid gritstone moorland above. The road also gives access to many famous pot-holes.

By following the Turbary Road down North End Scar, you reach a gate and a stile leading over into the next enclosure. Across the field the next stile can be seen on the skyline and this is our objective except that it is worth making a diversion up to the right to the prominent stand of trees. Here is to be found Marble Steps Pot, a huge rift in the ground, with an obvious stepped entrance; a giant's staircase leading into the bowels of the earth. It is possible for the daring to scramble down the entrance steps, but care is needed because the limestone can be greasy with rain and mud and the last 'step' is a very deep one indeed! It is an awesome place, so typical of the caves, gorges and pot-holes which festoon this fell. Only a short distance away from the Marble Steps are some enormous sink holes and in one of them you can see where cavers have been trying to open an entrance to the caves which must lie below.

After a look at the pot-hole it is an easy walk across the field to the next stile. Crossing the stile takes you out of the National Park and out of Yorkshire into Lancashire, for this is the boundary where white rose meets red rose.

The map calls this area Ireby Fell. It consists of a long, narrow wedge of fellside rising up towards Gragareth. There is a wall on either hand, and not just a wall, but a wall topped by barbed wire. In the distance, but well down from the summit, are the tall cairns for which this mountain, like Nine Standards Rigg or Wild Boar Fell, is famous. As you climb the fell—a relentless slope of tussock grass, over a mile long—the walls gradually come closer and

The walk crosses the Turbary Road, once used by peat gatherers.

decision has to be made.

The walk begins at a bend in the Kingsdale road near the place where the green lane from Twistleton Scar End comes in. A ladder stile leads over the wall and soon starts to climb the steep bank above where footholds have been worn in the turf like the steps kicked by climbers into snow slopes. Up above rises tier upon tier of shattered limestone in a typical Ingleton type of scar or outcrop, like a huge rock garden. It is like mounting a ladder up the steep turf but before long the first rock appears underfoot.

It really would make a marvellous rock garden! Easy scrambling leads up towards a ladder stile in the wall above the scar, but closer together, so that you begin to feel trapped like some wild beast being forced into a snare. You can't see the end until the last minute—and then it is too late. You actually *are* trapped! The walls come together in a short end wall and there is no stile.

This is what I can't understand. Why is there a fairly new stile leading over from Marble Steps Pot into Ireby Fell, if there's no way out? A stile is needed at the head of the field, but at present the only way ahead is to climb the wall in the corner where there are some convenient through-stones, and drop over to the left of the county boundary.

By following the county boundary wall the top of the fell is reached; a trig block accompanied by a curious ridge of peat like a frozen brown wave. The summit stands well away from the wall as if to declare itself firmly in the red rose camp!

What a view there is from the summit! The Howgills and Barbondale, Kirkby Lonsdale and the silver ribbon of the Lune river all the way to Lancaster, the great sweep of More-cambe Bay, the Lakeland Fells, Bowland, Ilkley Moor, Ingleborough and the Yorkshire fells. It is an astonishing panorama, the like of which is not matched anywhere else in this book.

But there's an end of it. This is not an onward walk or circular tour, for obvious reasons. It's back the way you came my lad, and don't let me catch you this way again!

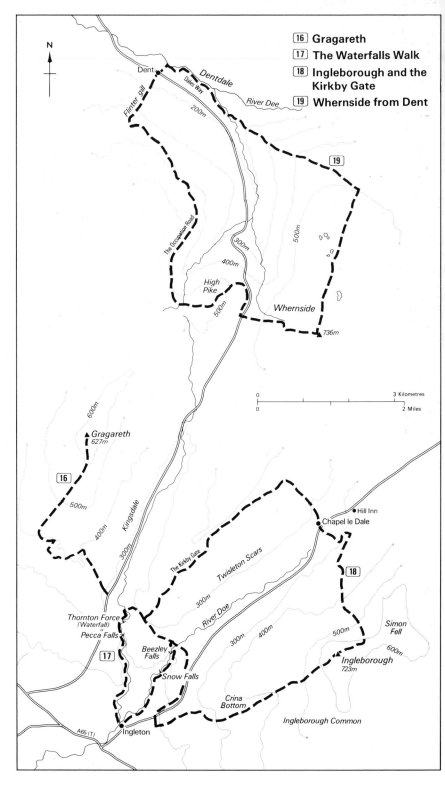

16 Gragareth
17 The Waterfalls Walk
18 Ingleborough and the Kirkby Gate
19 Whernside from Dent

WALK 17: The Waterfalls Walk

Thornton Force.

Map: Yorkshire Dales Western Area, 1:25,000.
Start: Car park at the foot of Thornton Beck. MR693734. Small entry charge.
Distance: 4¹/₂ miles.
Time: 2¹/₂ hours.
What's it Like?: The best *series* of waterfalls in Britain. Extremely popular. A great many concrete steps, environmentally insensitive, but probably necessary in view of the number of visitors. The steps are mostly unguarded; young children need careful watching or they could go for a long waterslide.
Shorter Alternative: Many visitors turn back at the refreshment hut just before Thornton Force, but this does not save much in distance and loses many of the best sights.
Bad Weather Alternative: Visit the show cave at White Scar MR713745.

Two Ingleton Glens and their Magnificent Waterfalls

The little town of Ingleton lies at the western edge of the Dales where the streams from Kingsdale and Chapel-le-dale meet to form the River Greta. It isn't a pretty place in the way that Clapham is, say, or some of the Wharfedale villages, but it is a fascinating one for all that. It has in the past tried to combine the functions of being a tourist centre and an industrial village, which is a difficult trick to pull off with any success, though Ingleton seems to have managed it. There was a mill down by the river (recently demolished to make way for some chic houses), a great quarry with limekilns which closed in 1909 and last but not least, a coalmine which didn't shut down until 1937.

The Pecca Twin Falls.

Tourism came with the railway from Skipton in 1849 and 12 years later a spectacular viaduct was built across the Greta to carry the line on to Lowgill where it joined the main Scottish rails of the London and North Western. There was a station at each end of the viaduct and during a period of rivalry between the LNWR, who controlled the northern half, and the Midland Railway, who controlled the southern half, passengers were forced to get off their train at one station, walk over the viaduct and get on another train in order to continue their journey! The viaduct remains but the rails have long since been torn up and nowadays nobody is allowed to walk across.

The North Craven Fault, which is responsible for the coal measures still being below Ingleton due to a massive slippage of the strata, is also responsible for the deep-lying Pre-Cambrian rocks being so near the surface in this area. It is important to appreciate this because this is what gives the Ingleton glens their unique features. In them the water has cut through the relatively thin limestone crust left by the faulting, down into the slates and other early rocks. It is quite easy to see this: the blue-grey sheen of the slate is readily distinguishable from the white limestone, and, to make it even clearer, the slate is vertically bedded against the limestone's horizontal bedding. There are places on the walk where this is so obvious you would have to be particularly dim not to notice it. It affects the walk in another way, too. Because one rock is alkaline (limestone) and the other acidic, the plant growth varies accordingly. Where the limestone predominates the woods are of ash, hazel and yew; where the slates are to the fore the oaks take over. Sometimes there seems a bit of a mix up, with lime-loving plants growing in an obviously slatey area—but that's a little puzzle I'll leave you to sort out for yourselves! For anyone who walks with their eyes open and senses sharpened, this trip is utterly fascinating.

It is hardly surprising that the two glens have been popular with tourists from time immemorial. In earlier days the glens were separately owned and touts would greet each tourist train, extolling the virtues of one glen against the other. Then, as now, there was an entrance fee. To make the glens more accessible the paths were improved, bridges built and walks created which were the very epitome of Victorian romantic scenery. Such 'improved' glens, chines and gorges were immensely popular at that time, and though there are several examples still to be found in the Alps, the Ingleton glens may be the last notable example in Britain.

That they should still be popular in this sophisticated age is really quite remarkable, but popular they certainly are. This is not a walk for anyone who wants to be alone with Nature; all the world and his dog come this way, especially on a Bank Holiday. Yet despite the popularity, despite the 'improvements', this is not a walk to be missed.

The walk begins at the Old Bridge on the western edge of the village, below the church, where there's a piece of nondescript ground with the Black and White Cafe on it and beyond that the ticket hut giving admittance to the walk. There's a car park here, guarded by the buttresses of the old single track railway which once served Mealbank Quarry, but this is soon left behind and a good path wanders into the Swilla Glen where the river runs on a flat, stony bed and the limestone walls of the gorge, though obscured by trees, can be glimpsed soaring up to the sky.

According to the Ordnance Survey the river we are following is the Twiss, otherwise known as the Thornton Beck or the Kingsdale Beck, and the river of our return will be the Doe, alias Chapel Beck or Dale Beck. But the Ordnance Survey got it wrong, for what they call the Twiss should be the Doe and vice versa—pretty obvious really when you learn that the valley of Chapel-le-dale is also called Twisleton Dale. The fault is a long-standing one which the Ordnance Survey seem reluctant to admit, with the result that confusion now reigns and the only thing everyone agrees about is that the two rivers join at the railway viaduct and become the Greta!

Soon the valley narrows and a footbridge leads across the stream. The sound of rushing water becomes quite distinct and in a minute or two another footbridge is reached which gives a view upstream of a wonderful waterfall, the Pecca Falls. Concrete steps twist up by the falls, following the narrow gorge and steps like these are to be a feature throughout the walk, appearing as the occasion demands—usually steep and unguarded. The gill is here at its most picturesque as a series of waterfalls unfolds, notably Pecca Twin and Hollybush Spout, and then quite suddenly the path bursts out into the open and climbs up to the brow of a hill where there is a refreshment hut serving tea and other goodies.

Beyond the hut the path follows the stream through an open valley towards the principal

waterfall of the tour, Thornton Force. It is a broad flow, pouring over a lip some forty feet above a bowl in the hills. The meeting of the limestone and the older slate, known as unconformity, can be seen very clearly at Thornton Force and it is safe enough to approach these rocks and try out Arthur Raistrick's famous dictum that at Thornton Force the span of a hand can encompass three million years.

Beyond the Force the path climbs steeply to a bend in the river known as Raven Ray (there are some very curious names along these streams) and to a footbridge which gives access to an old 'green lane'. This leads to the buildings at Scar End where a fine vista opens up across Chapel-le-dale to Ingleborough; that singular mountain which stands as proud as any in the land. It always reminds me of a badly-made wedding cake with the third tier removed, and the last time I saw it from Scar End, wisps of light cloud were drifting across its top giving it an unwanted air of mystery.

The view of the peak from here is one of the best there is. Quite distinct, too, are the buildings and flagpole of the White Scar Caves; a showcave which can easily be reached from this point.

From Scar End a footpath leads across a meadow to Oddie's Lane, which is the old Roman Road up Chapel-le-dale, straight as an arrow and now surfaced. The signpost to Beezley Falls directs us across the road and down to the farm of the same name where the stepping stones across the river can clearly be seen (you can get to White Scar Caves that way), though our route takes us in a different direction, across a field and into a thickly wooded gorge.

The path descends the gorge quite steeply past a series of magnificent waterfalls constituting the Beezley Falls and Rival Falls. If anything the situation is even more enchanting than the Thornton Beck; the rocks, the trees and the water combine to form a picture like a Chinese painting. In my opinion, the view upstream at the Triple Spout of Beezley Falls is the best of the whole trip.

Below these falls the stream has cut an extremely deep slot in the rock called Baxenghyll Gorge where the viewing platform—a bridge over the stream—is unfortunately now barred to access, so it can't be seen to the best advantage. Here as elsewhere there is always the temptation to use the natural rocks which overhang these rivers throughout their length in order to get a closer look and some foolhardy souls do teeter over the abyss either out of curiosity or daring, despite the many warning signs. As a result there have been numerous accidents over the years and not a few deaths.

Below the gorge is the curiously named Snow Falls after which the path becomes much less steep, passes some old quarries and emerges from the woods at Skerwith Beck. (There's another waterfall on this beck called Cat Leap Force; 30ft high and missed by the majority of visitors.) But now the vale is broad and the path becomes a bridleway. The skeletal remains of old quarry buildings appear and across the valley, Meal Bank Quarry itself, largely overgrown.

The way leads straight to the heart of the village and it only remains to walk down the street past the church and back to the car.

Far left: **Rival Falls on the River Twiss.**

Above: **Raven Ray is the name given to Thornton Beck's dale above the force.**

WALK 18: Ingleborough and the Kirkby Gate

Ingleborough and the cottage at Crina Bottom.

Map: Yorkshire Dales Western Area, 1:25,000.
Start: Where Fell Lane meets the Hawes road, MR702731. Adequate parking. After a period of heavy rain it might be preferable to start from Skirwith (MR707737) because this cuts out some of the muddiest parts of Fell Lane. It also saves about 30 minutes on the day, but the parking is limited to a couple of cars and in good weather the original start is nicer anyway.
Distance: 11 miles.
Time: 5 hours.
What's it Like?: One of the traditional ways of climbing the Dales' finest mountain, with a return which offers very extensive panoramas. The descent of Ingleborough is steep and needs care, as does the descent of Twistleton Scar End to a lesser degree, though neither is very fearsome. Kirkby Gate is not always easy to follow and Fell Lane, in its lower part, can be very muddy in wet weather.

Shorter Alternative: Climb the mountain and return by the same way—about 3 hours or less. See text.
Bad Weather Alternative: Visit the show cave at White Scar, MR713745.

Chapel le Dale and Twistleton Scars

There can be no denying the fact that the most dominant mountain in the whole of the Yorkshire Dales is Ingleborough, a huge bulk of a hill rising proudly above the village of Ingleton, singular in form and mass. Ingleborough has a tiered structure, like a badly-made wedding cake and because it rises in virtual isolation, cut off from the other peaks by deep valleys, its striking form can be seen for miles around, immediately identifiable.

There are several ways of climbing Ingleborough but one of the most popular, and deservedly so, is the direct route from Ingleton via Fell Lane and Crina Bottom. It is simple, easy to follow and very beautiful.

The walk starts out of the village along the Hawes road, a few yards past the junction with the old road to Clapham. Here there is an area of open ground where it is possible to park.

A bridleway leads up to a corner where it becomes a walled green lane climbing gently towards the White Scars, an area of Great Scar Limestone which underlies the grit of the upper mountain and shows itself here as typical small crags, with sink holes, pot holes and all the paraphernalia of limestone country. In the sunlight it gleams pure white like a toothpaste advert.

The lane can be muddy because it is rutted by tractor tyres but it is not too bad. There are views, looking back, over the village and the wide country beyond, limited by the distant moors of Bowland Forest. At a turn in the lane, Ingleborough bursts into view, gradually becoming more prominent as the lane climbs up a rise to Crina Bottom. There's a farm here, isolated in a sleepy hollow with a few trees and backed by low limestone cliffs, while the great mountain glowers overhead, shadowed perhaps by a passing cloud. It is a lovely scene, and perhaps the best of all the views of Ingleborough.

Beyond Crina Bottom the lane degrades into a track and the hard work begins. It looks steep and it is steep; a steady grind over blocks of millstone grit with, near the top, the two very steep steps which give the mountain its distinctive profile. Suddenly a cairn heaves into view, then another, and you are on the summit plateau. It is only a few steps to the trig block (723m, 2372ft).

The summit plateau of Ingleborough is quite enormous. It is like a flat parade ground covered with cobblestones—except that they are not cobbles but small gritstones. Various cairns and windbreaks are scattered about and there are even remnants of the ancient fort where the Brigantes defied the Romans. As a

Ingleborough in winter. The mountain dominates the scene for miles around. (Photo: Duncan Unsworth.)

fort it must have been fairly impregnable,
though it is doubtful whether the Brigantes
occupied it permanently—there's no water
near enough and anyway, in winter everyone
would have died of exposure!

It takes about one and a half hours to climb
Ingleborough this way and you could reckon
an hour in descent, or say a three-hour round
trip, giving time to observe the view and
investigate the plateau before returning. To
continue the walk, however, we cross the
plateau and descend the steep rocky slopes
leading down to the col between Ingleborough
and Simon Fell. A well-known spring emerges
on the col and carves a precipitous course
down the north face; it is remarkable how this
stream develops from nothing to a swift and
bubbling beck in a matter of a few yards. By
the side of the stream a very steep path
descends, broken into a thousand ledges and
not at all easy going. I once saw an elderly
couple descending here, carrying a dog
apiece—that'll teach 'em to bring corgis on a
mountain!

Humphrey Bottom, below the slope, is
reached with a certain degree of relief, but it
doesn't last long because the path becomes
very boggy and unpleasant. Lower down it is
so bad that duckboards have been laid,
otherwise you would be up to your fetlocks in
slime. It is only for three quarters of a mile or
so that the bog is at its worst and once the
Great Scar Limestone is reached all is sweet-
ness and light again. The limestone here is very
fine and worth examining.

Down past Braithwaite Wife Hole, a huge
depression in the rock and on improving paths
to the buildings at Souther Scales and so to the
motor road. Alternatively, the path can be
followed half a mile further to come out on the
road a few yards from the Hill Inn, one of the
traditional watering holes for walkers,
climbers and cavers in the Dales.

Across the road from where the path
emerges there is the entrance to a narrow
surfaced road called Oddie's Lane which
follows the line of the old Roman Road to
Ingleton. The lane leads in a short distance to
the hamlet of Chapel-le-Dale and the tiny
chapel of St. Leonard, where there is a

Chapel le Dale, with Whernside in the background.

memorial tablet to the men who died constructing the railway between Settle and Dent Head. They are buried here, in this tiny hamlet, and the railway company paid to have the churchyard extended to hold them.

By the side of the church a surfaced bridleway climbs gently uphill, past the deep and gloomy Hurdle Pot, shaded by trees. It is ten metres to the water at the bottom of the hole, where the sun can scarcely ever penetrate and where black trout are said to live! Hurdle Pot also has a boggart, or evil spirit, who tempts unwary walkers to their doom, so pass by carefully!

A bit further on and you might think the boggart has escaped from the hole and is standing by the side of the lane, but the startling object turns out to be a piece of modern sculpture done by the artist Charles l'Anson and placed here by the owner of Gillhead, the charming white house at the head of the lower lane. A few years ago vandals actually did toss the sculpture into Hurdle Pot, but cavers retrieved and restored it

The trees and the bulbs which decorate the lane in spring are also part of the Gillhead influence and soon the house itself is passed; an ancient farm, long and low and painted white. Beyond Gillhead the lane winds up towards Ellerbeck farm, through an area of shake holes, symptomatic of the region, until at the Ellerbeck ford it meets a path known as Kirkby Gate.

A 'gate' is a street, the word derived from the Old Norse, so this was obviously a well-trodden footpath to Ingleton and, ultimately, Kirkby Lonsdale, in the old days. It runs almost dead straight across Twistleton Scars, hard to follow in places now, because it is not worn at all. It can be boggy at first, but then, when it reaches the limestone pavement, it is virtually untraceable.

On a clear day the problem is resolved by heading for the large cairn which can be seen on the horizon. With luck the path will reappear—in fact it may come and go several times before it finally gathers itself together and marches unmistakably towards the limes-

An unusual sink hole on Kirkby Gate.

tone horizon where there is a distinct nick or 'door'. In bad weather a bit of nifty compass work is the best answer. For those without a compass, however, the tendency is always to wander too far left, but by deliberately keeping to the right a guide in the form of a wall can be used which will lead you more or less to the place which is wanted.

It is very strange that there is no name for the gap in the rocks, because it is so very distinctive. It ought to be called Twistleton Nick. It is certainly as distinctive as Sulber Nick, on Ingleborough (See Walk 20).

All the way along Kirkby Gate there are wonderful views of Ingleborough, Whernside and the great railway viaduct at Ribblehead.

For these last two you have to turn round and look back, but that is a trick any experienced walker has acquired over the years. In the case of Whernside it is well worth observing how it changes shape as you travel along parallel with its axis, which is what the Kirkby Gate does.

Through Twistleton Nick, fresh vistas open out. Ingleton lies below, the Wenning Valley in the middle distance and beyond that the brooding fells of Bowland; the Lancashire witch country.

From Twistleton Nick it is steeply down to Beezley's farm and the stepping stones over the river. Soon the Hawes road is reached at Skirwith, through the quarry drive, and it is only a few minutes' walk back to the car.

WALK 19: Whernside from Dent

Map: Yorkshire Dales Western Area, 1:25,000.
Start: Car park at the entrance to Dent Town from Sedbergh, MR704871.
Distance: 12 miles.
Time: 6 hours.
What's it Like?: A superb walk in the grand manner sweeping round Deepdale. The start is very steep and the Occupation Road seems very long. In bad weather accurate navigation is required on Whernside, especially in descent.
Shorter Alternatives: These are mentioned in the text and are classic walks in their own right: 1) Descend by Nun House Outrake and follow the river back to Dent Town, (5 miles); 2) Descend by the path through Deepdale from the Kingsdale road and join the above route at Mill Bridge, (9 miles).
Bad Weather Alternatives: Dent is a delightful place to potter. The church is worth a visit and there are several studios—craft, photography and John Cooke, the well known artist. This place is the Clovelly of the north—extremely popular and on a hot summer Sunday you keep tripping over amateur painters busy at work.

Climbing the Highest Fell

The honour of being the highest fell in the Yorkshire Dales belongs not to the handsome Ingleborough as is often thought, but to its neighbour Whernside. At 736m (2415ft), Whernside tops Ingleborough by 13m (43ft).

It is climbed as one of the famous Yorkshire Three Peaks (See Walk 21) from Ribblehead by way of Batty Green and Little Dale and this is by far the most popular route. From Dent, however, Whernside is just the highlight of a much finer walk which sweeps round the fells

The Occupation Road near Flinter Gill, above Dent.

Dent Town.

above Deepdale in a most commanding manner.

The walk begins at the car park on the western edge of Dent Town (I don't see why lovely old Dent with its twisting cobbled streets should be denied its ancient name). Across the road from the car park a short lane leads to the village green at the far corner of which there is a leafy narrow lane twisting uphill past an old non-conformist chapel. At first the lane is surfaced but soon the tarmac gives way to rough stones as it climbs remorsely. It is called Flintergill Lane and it is so steep it is hard to credit that it was once an important pack-horse track between Dent and Lancaster. Flintergill itself splashes away on the left of the track, often in a miniature gorge, thickly wooded.

Flintergill climbs 750ft in half a mile, give or take a step or two, and it takes about twenty minutes. At the top it breaks out of the trees and joins another stony lane at a T-junction. The new lane is called Occupation Road. It is a remarkable affair in that it contours round the fellsides below Great Coum for five and a half miles from Barbondale (MR679862) to Deepdale Head (MR723823) climbing slightly the while. It was made in 1859 to service the enclosures which were only just being implemented in Dent at that late date. It was used by carriers from some of the famous Dent Marble quarries and it probably incorporated the old jaggers' track to Lancaster mentioned earlier.

From the junction there is a superb view of the Howgills over to the north-west. Yarlside is the dominant peak—a distinctly pointed cone rising from the deep Cautley Holme Beck. Dentdale runs below our feet and across it is the steep sided Aye Gill Pike which separates the valley from Garsdale, then the eye sweeps round east to the huge bulk of Great Knoutberry Hill (672m, 2205ft) at the very head of Dentdale and the most distant Great Shunner Fell (716m, 2349ft).

We follow the Occupation Road south-east towards Deepdale Head. At first it is very stony until, after about a mile, it meets another junction (MR711846), where a lane called Nun House Outrake descends swiftly to the dale bottom at High Nun House. By descending here, and joining the last mile or so of the full walk, it is possible to enjoy a round trip of 5 miles which is in itself one of the classic walks of the Dales.

But for us there is sterner stuff. The old road, never less than 30ft wide, becomes a green lane and a very boggy green lane at that. After a long period of wet weather keep off the Occy Road, as the locals call it. In dry weather it isn't perhaps too bad—certainly there are worse—but as is so often the case with these old bridal ways, the surface has been irreparably damaged by tractors and trial bikes.

Up on the right, the fellside slopes to the summit of Great Coum (687m, 2254ft), which is quite a shapely mountain, with a little ring of crags and one or two of those rather odd stone men which seem scattered on the fells between here and Mallerstang and of which Nine Standards Rigg is best known, (see Walk 8). About this time Whernside, which has been in view for most of the day, begins to seem a distant goal and a very steep one to boot, but never fear—things are not as bad as they seem.

Here and there are little quarries like the one at Binks (MR708836) where the limestone known as Dent Marble was excavated during the 19th century. It made fashionable fireplaces which were sent all over the kingdom.

As the lane winds round the head of the Gastack Beck the dull slopes of Gragareth come into view and in the distance, proud Ingleborough.

At last, however, the Occupation Road reaches Deepdale Head where it joins the surfaced road running from Dent to Ingleton through Kingsdale. This place is the actual summit of the col between Deepdale and Kingsdale, 468m (1535ft) above sea level. Since Whernside, which lies directly above, is 736m (2415ft), the climb now facing the walker is a mere 268m or 880ft. This is encouraging news and further encouragement is gained from the fact that the way ahead doesn't look *too* steep. The fellside seems to lie back, comfortingly.

However, here again is an opportunity to opt out of the full walk. By turning left along the surfaced road a path can soon be found on the right of the road which leads down Deepdale and rejoins our route near Mill Bridge. This too is a popular walk.

Once more, however, we must set our face to sterner things. The way to go is along the fence which shoots straight up from the road. The path is best described as tenuous, though it does improve higher up. It scarcely matters. Up ahead there is a curious neb of scree and this is the first target, perhaps a bit steeper than you imagined in your earlier euphoria, but taking only some twenty minutes of effort. After that, you've cracked it.

Only at this stage does it become apparent that Whernside is built like one of those old fashioned sand castles children used to make

on the beach with a big bucketful of sand, then a smaller bucketful perched on top of it. On this side at least (but not the other, let me add) there is a wide shelf between the bottom bit and the top bit where one can catch one's breath. By aiming for the hogsback skyline (the path is over on the right but again, it doesn't matter) you fetch up at the trig block, the summit of Whernside (736m, 2415ft).

As you would expect from the highest of all vantage points, the view is wide ranging. Ingleborough, as always, steals the show—it really is the most intrusive of mountains—but the view extends way over to Bowland on the one hand and the Lakeland fells on the other. The Duddon estuary can be seen quite clearly on a bright day.

The trig block is by the side of a wall which has a couple of well-made gaps in it and a notice saying quite firmly that the path is on the other side! And so it is; a dark trodden line running along the summit ridge, which we now follow to the north. On the left is a new stoutly-made wire fence marking the boundary of a Euro Constituency (as if anyone cared—I hope Brussels paid for the fence) and on the right is a very steep drop down to the glinting waters of Greensett Moss. I once came up that way and you can take it from me it is every bit as steep as it looks! Between the fence and the drop the ridge is narrow.

Suddenly the Euro fence takes a sharp bend to the right and the track follows it, but we leave it at this point and climb over the fence by means of a stile. In the distance you can see the Whernside Tarns—how many depends on the dryness of the season—resting on the

northern end of the great shelf I spoke about earlier. Here it forms a mini plateau. There is no path to speak of but a curious block of millstone grit, symbolic of the mountain, is a good target to aim for. Whernside means the place of millstones and this particular part of the fell is known as Mill Stone Brow. From there it is only minutes to the edge of the largest tarn. Few places in the Dales are more lonely than this; the sky and the moors are given another dimension by this bleak pool. In the far distance Yarlside still sticks up in the Howgills like a sore thumb and makes a good guidepost because by walking towards it you are on the correct line of descent.

Dentdale gradually spreads out below like a map. On the left is a great cairn and ruined hut and below is a series of old intakes whose walls are ruinous too. Our way goes straight down past the intakes to a distinct path traversing round the mountain side. This is the Great Wold, or Craven Way, an ancient packhorse route from Dent to Ingleton. It becomes a green lane and descends quite steeply into Deepdale near Whernside Manor, the national caving centre.

Back in the dale bottom the character of the walk changes yet again. By going along the road for a few minutes, Mill Bridge is reached where Deepdale Beck comes trickling down. A footpath follows the beck to its junction with the River Dee, then follows that stream to Church Bridge at the entrance to Dent Town. After the high moors it makes quite a change to wander the last couple of miles through lush meadows where in spring the hawthorn scent lies heavy on the air.

Far left: **The start of Flinter Gill at Dent.**

Middle: **The summit of Whernside.**

Above: **A gentle stroll along the Dee into Dent Town ends the walk.**

WALK 20: Ingleborough from Clapham

Ingleborough from the path above Trow Gill.

Map: Yorkshire Dales Western Area, 1:25,000.
Start: Car park at Clapham MR746693. Clapham also has a railway station on the Leeds-Lancaster line at MR733677, about a mile from the village.
Distance: 11 miles.
Time: 7 hours.
What's it Like?: This is one of the most interesting and varied walks in Britain, especially for geologists. Because of this the time given above should be regarded as minimal. Route finding can be tricky in mist, in particular round the Sulber Nick area, otherwise the going is not too bad.
Shorter Alternatives: A great many including: 1) Return by the Clapham Lane—Long Lane variant (see text). Saves about an hour; 2) Walk up Crummackdale (with or without visiting the Norber erratics) and return via Clapham Lane

and Long Lane (3 hrs); 3) Gaping Gill and back (3 hrs).
Bad Weather Alternatives: Visit either Ingleborough Cave, or Settle with its Museum of North Craven Life, swimming pool, shops, etc.

A Geological Wonderland

Ingleborough was once thought to be the highest mountain in England. This is not really surprising because it does dominate its surroundings—and not only its immediate surroundings, for it can be seen from miles away, especially in the west. It is isolated by deep and wide valleys from its fellow mountains and it has a distinctive shape. Of course, far from being the highest mountain in England, it isn't even the highest in the Dales—the adjacent Whernside is 13m higher.

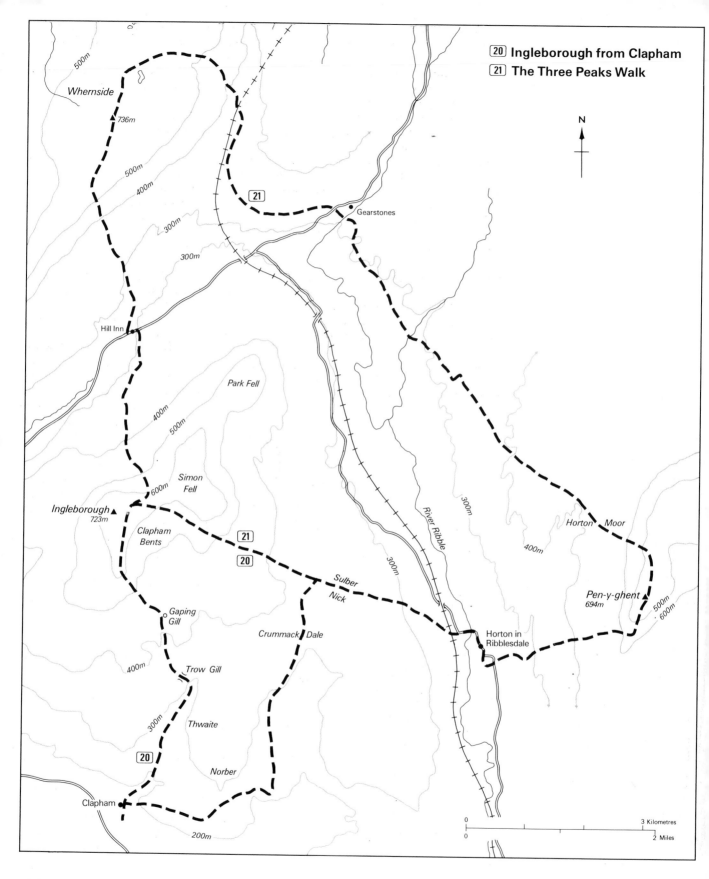

20 **Ingleborough from Clapham**
21 **The Three Peaks Walk**

N

Whernside

736m

500m

500m

400m

300m

300m

Gearstones

Hill Inn

Park Fell

400m

500m

Simon
Fell

600m

River Ribble

Horton Moor

300m

Ingleborough
723m

Clapham
Bents

21

20

Sulber
Nick

300m

400m

Pen-y-ghent
694m

500m

600m

Gaping
Gill

Crummack Dale

Horton in
Ribblesdale

400m

Trow Gill

300m

Thwaite

20

Norber

Clapham

200m

0   3 Kilometres

0   2 Miles

Nevertheless, despite this fall from grace, Ingleborough lives up to its promise. It is the most fascinating mountain in the Dales and the ascent from the village of Clapham is the most fascinating of all.

The old grey village straggles on either side of the Clapham Beck, one half linked to the other by three bridges including an ancient footbridge of arching limestone. The church is at the top end and the pub at the bottom and in between, tucked away, is the large car park and information centre of the National Park where this walk commences.

The route leaves the village past the church to enter on the former grounds of Ingleborough Hall. The Hall itself is behind the church and is now an outdoor pursuits centre, but it was for many years the home of the Farrer family, whose most celebrated member was Reginald John Farrer, the famous plant hunter and the man who more than anyone else made rock gardens so immensely popular. His alpine garden at the Hall was world famous. Farrer brought back plants from China, Tibet and Japan as well as the Alps before he died in Burma in 1920, aged 40.

The way into the grounds is through the old sawmill (small charge) which gives access to a wide carriageway called Clapdale Drive, that runs by the side of an artificial lake created by the Farrers in the 1830s. All round the lake, and some way beyond, are the trees planted by the Farrers; the beech, larch and yew, the silver fir and here and there something more exotic brought back from China or Tibet. In season bluebells and wild garlic carpet the ground between the trees.

Clapham Beck tumbles into the lake at the far end and after about a half an hour's walk the path, climbing steadily, passes the entrance to Ingleborough Cave, a show cave open to the public. Beck Head is here, too; a spring issuing water which comes off the moor via Gaping Gill. Beyond this the path is rougher and there is a sense of impending drama as the limestone dale narrows and bends dramatically to the left. On the left, though you have to look for it, is Dead Man's Cave where a clothed skeleton was found in 1947. Local legend says it was a Nazi agent who had parachuted in during the war and lost his way, but the mystery has never been solved. Great walls of rock soar up and the dale narrows to a slot whose base is filled with a scree slope. This is Trow Gill and it is a magical place, full of adventure and mystery and beloved by kids of all ages.

Climbing the scree brings one out into a green upper valley, very shallow, which in turn climbs onto the moor and leads to the great pothole of Gaping Gill, perhaps the most celebrated specimen of its genre in England. From the surface the pothole is rather disappointing, for it simply consists of a nondescript slot down which Fell Beck empties, like rainwater down a grid. It's a sobering thought, though, that Fell Beck is plunging twice the height of Niagara, for Gaping Gill is 365ft deep.

Below the surface slot the pothole opens into a magnificent chamber and at the spring and summer bank holiday weekends local pothole clubs operate a winch and bosun's chair which will lower you to the bottom in a jiffy. This costs nothing. There is, however, a charge for bringing you back up again!

Gaping Gill was first descended by the French cave explorer Martel in 1895. As mentioned earlier, the water from the cave comes to the surface at Beck Head, near Ingleborough Cave in Clapdale.

From the Gill there's a good view of Ingleborough, looking like a couchant lion, with the main summit as the head, and a

Trow Gill.

shallow dip for the small of the back before rising again to Simon Fell, the lion's rump. A good path takes you up slopes which are gentle at first, then suddenly steep, to the cairn on Little Ingleborough which lies in front of the Lion's head and is a convenient way up. A bit like crawling up the mane, really, for the path curls round to the neck of the beast then joins the main track along the rocky ridge to the top (723m, 2372ft).

The top of the mountain is a plateau with a huge windbreak and an extensive view which takes in Bowland and the Lakes as well as the Dales. The seminal position of the peak is made crystal clear, in case there was ever doubt about the matter.

From the summit the way down is back along the ridge to the well-marked path which swings off to the right, curling round the breast of Simon Fell. This is the popular way up from Horton and from its top end it looks like a ribbon tossed across the flank of the fell. The eye can trace it for almost its entire length.

Down then, past the old shooting hut, to an area of limestone scars, outcropping in fantastic array. The path leads through the rocks until it comes to a crossroads, beyond which there is a distinctive feature best described as a rock avenue and known as Sulber Nick. That is the way to Horton in Ribblesdale, but our route turns right at the crossroads, making for Crummackdale.

There are two routes possible from here and it is easy to mistake one route for the other in the mist. The chief path is a fine green lane, Clapham Lane, which leads back across the unenclosed Long Scar towards the head of Clapdale. There an ancient and rough bridleway called Long Lane, keeping well above the woods and lake on the east side, descends to the village of Clapham. This route offers fine views of Thwaite Scars, Trow Gill and—like black trolls on the skyline—some of the Norber erratics. It is a good way back, perhaps on a second visit or if time is pressing, because it is shorter than the route I am about to describe.

At Sulber Gate it is best to go slightly to the left and cross an amphitheatre of limestone clints towards a line of cliffs where there is a way down known as Beggar's Stile. This gives access to Crummackdale, a short but broad valley of incredible bleakness. I first came upon it one raw winter's day of mizzle and mist and the impression it made on me was unforgettable. It was like Hell frozen over.

There is only one dwelling in the valley,

Trow Gill.

Crummack Farm. A stream, Austwick Beck, issues from a slot in the rocks and wanders down the valley bottom, which is bare of trees. Over on the eastern edge of the valley are crags and scars in great profusion in an area called Moughton (pronounced Mooton). These circle round the valley head and are continued on the west side by the Thwaite Scars. There seems to be limestone everywhere, in clints and grikes, crags and scars.

The path leads straight to the farm and from there a farm lane, Crummack Lane, travels down the valley. Where it turns sharply right there is a path leading off it towards Norber Brow and the line of limestone cliffs. By following this above the cliffs you come upon the Norber Boulders, perhaps the best example of erratics in Britain. These black Silurian blocks were plucked from deep beds in Crummackdale by an Ice Age glacier which then dumped them on top of Norber Brow.

There's a good view from the Brow too, of the Wenning Valley and the hills beyond, but the path returns below the scar to a wide field which it crosses diagonally to a stile giving access to Thwaite Lane, an ancient bridleway. This leads back to Clapham. The final curiosity of a walk which is full of curiosities, comes right at the end when the path plunges into a tunnel. A railway tunnel perhaps? No, when the Farrers built their estate they didn't want a common right of way running through their back garden, so to speak, so they built the garden *over* the path. You could do things like that in those days if you were lord of the manor!

WALK 21: The Three Peaks Walk

Pen-y-ghent is the first of the Three Peaks to be tackled – it is traversed from right to left as seen in this picture.

Map: Yorkshire Dales Western Area, 1:25,000.
Start: Car park in Horton in Ribblesdale MR808726.
Distance: 22 miles.
Time: 9 – 12 hours depending on conditions. 10 hours is about average. It is usual to 'clock in' at the Pen-y-ghent Café before setting out and on return. Anyone who does the walk inside the 12 hours is then invited to join the Three Peaks Club and receive a badge. Badges are not available except to successful members.
What's it Like?: This is one of the great classic fell-walks of Britain. Experienced walkers will not find it unduly arduous: most people agree that Whernside is the toughest challenge of the three peaks, and the long leg between Pen-y-ghent and Whernside sometimes seems never-ending!
Shorter Alternatives: Individual routes up Whernside and Ingleborough are given in Walks

18–20. Alas, there seems no alternative way up Pen-y-ghent that would help reduce erosion.
Bad Weather Alternative: Visit the White Scar Cave above Ingleton or the museum at Settle.

Around Ribblehead

To compile a book about the classic walks of the Yorkshire Dales and not include the Three Peaks Walk would be like trying to write Hamlet and leaving out the Prince. And yet there is such a pressure on this route, so many boots, that one is reluctant to encourage more. What should be a joyous celebration of a very fine walk becomes inevitably tinged with a certain sadness. A good deal of thought by the National Park authorities is being put into ameliorating the problem of human erosion here and this will be a continuing process for some years, either by altering the route from time to time or reinforcing parts of it with nylon mesh and the like. No less than 50km is earmarked for treatment. What follows is a general description—alas, the path is so worn there is no problem following the route itself on the ground.

The Three Peaks in question are Pen-y-ghent (694m, 2277ft), Whernside (736m, 2415ft), and Ingleborough (723m, 2372ft). They form a triangular route round the head of Ribblesdale, symbolised by the great Ribblehead viaduct of the Settle–Carlisle railway line which stretches out so commandingly across Batty Moss. They are usually tackled in the order I have given them, starting from the village of Horton in Ribblesdale.

From Horton a lane leads to Brackenbottom and from there a well marked track crosses Brackenbottom Scar to the foot of Pen-y-ghent which it climbs by way of the prominent rocky nose. This is a delightful ascent, a bit scrambly but somewhat marred nowadays by the state of the track. It is quite steep to climb, but the ascent does not last long and the top is soon reached. This is psychologically important, for reaching the first summit so soon is a great boost to the confidence!

From the trig block our way passes through a gate in the summit wall. Horton Moor stretches out below, undulating and endless to the distant bulk of Whernside, and the euphoria of a moment ago is tempered by the sheer distance of it all. It is a fact that it is not the three mountains themselves which get blamed for failure to complete the course, but this long slog across the moors between Pen-y-ghent and Whernside. It is so—*sapping*.

There are big crags on the left, unsuspected from where we stand on the top of Pen-y-ghent, so in bad weather especially, a modicum of care is called for. The route sweeps down and across the moor to High Birkwith Farm (MR801768) and then to Nether Lodge (MR794778). From there the route used to drop down to the valley road, B6479, which was followed to Ribblehead, from where a farm track led to Winterscales and a more or less direct ascent of Whernside. But this way is no longer recommended and a good job too—the road walk was incredibly boring and the ascent of Whernside from Winterscales was steep, muddy and extremely fatiguing. The track became so worn that eventually the authorities closed it.

There was always an alternative which the more discerning walkers took—a right of way across the fields from Nether Lodge to Gearstones, on the B6255, Hawes road (MR780800). This part of the walk is extremely pleasant and does a lot to ameliorate the long moorland slog between the two peaks. Gearstones itself used to be an old drovers' inn which finally closed its doors in 1911. It is difficult to imagine that in this bleak place there was actually a weekly corn market until about 1870!

Across the road from Gearstones the moors

Winter grips the rocks of Ingleborough. (Photo: Duncan Unsworth.)

The Three Peaks is a tough walk in winter. Whernside seen from Ingleborough. (Photo: Duncan Unsworth.)

are decorated with a number of low but attractive limestone scars and the most satisfactory way of doing the next bit of the walk is to follow these in the general direction of the great Ribblehead viaduct. What an impressive monument to Victorian engineering this viaduct is! The land in front of the viaduct is Batty Green where there once stood the most important of the labour camps used to house workers during the construction of the railway. Some 2000 souls lived here and the camp had a school, hospital, post office and library. The railway was completed in 1876 and is one of the most scenic in Britain—whether it will survive the harsh economics of the late 20th century remains to be seen.

There is no path across the scars but by following the lie of the land, curving round with the natural shape of the moors, you drop down to Littledale by the side of the railway just before it plunges into the Bleamoor Tunnel. There's a rough path here which crosses the railway in the company of a stream by means of a curious aqueduct and then starts

its long traverse across the moors to Dent. This is the Craven Way or Great Wold, an old jaggers' track from Dent to Ingleton (See Walk 19). On the left is the deep little Force Gill and if you still have the energy you can make a diversion to see the fine waterfall (MR758820).

Before long a path leads off to the left and climbs steeply up the hill by the side of a stout wire fence, then follows the rather narrow crest of the mountain to its summit. It's a fine climb—much better than the old way—with exciting views down the steep east face to Greensett Moss and its tarn. It looks incredibly boggy down there and you can take it from me, it is!

The summit trig block lies behind a wall on Whernside, though two gaps have been specially created so that those who insist on laying their hands on the actual top can undertake their ritual fetish. Then the way leads steeply down the south ridge until, at the third steep drop of the ridge, a track plunges off to the left, down the flanks of the fell, to the farm at Bruntscar (MR738789). A farm lane leads to the road and the welcome Hill Inn.

This pub is extremely popular with walkers and cavers—the local equivalent of the Padarn or Dungeon Ghyll—and at one time the Three Peaks Walk actually started from here. It still can, of course, since it is a circular route, but most walkers like to get the crossing between Pen-y-ghent and Whernside out of their system early on and Horton has for some time been favourite.

Behind the inn a path leads up through attractive limestone scenery to a pothole with the curious name of Braithwaite Wife Hole. Whether this indicates some tragedy of long ago or whether Braithwaite used it as a means of keeping domestic control, is not known. The path crosses extremely boggy ground towards the frowning face of Ingleborough, here all steep crags and nasty scree. By this time, of course, you have knocked off a few miles (and if the Hill was open, perhaps a few pints) so the thought of climbing such steep places seems appalling. But it isn't too bad really. The path up the scree slopes on the left of the crags is steep but short and before you know it you are scrambling up the rough track from the saddle between Simon Fell and Ingleborough to the top of the latter.

There is a large windbreak on the summit and the remains of ancient fortifications, for this was the centre of the Venutian revolt, when the leader of the Brigantes, Venutius, defied the Roman legions for some years before they crushed him in 74AD. Marvellously defensive as it doubtless was, the summit of Ingleborough must have been a cold billet for Venutius and his lads.

The view is extensive over the Dales and Bowland, but I think it lacks the contrast of the view from Whernside.

And now it's downhill all the way! By retreating to the saddle again a good track can be seen curving round the flanks of Simon Fell to the clints and grikes of Sulber. Down and down, swiftly and easily, until at a cross-roads a sharp turn to the left enters on the strange formation known as Sulber Nick. This is a natural gap in the limestone; a God-made green lane which is a perfect end to this wonderful hill walk.

All that remains is to walk past the grim Beecroft Quarry and over the railway line to the Crown Inn and the car.

Above: **Gearstones – once a lonely inn.**

Above left: **Whernside from Batty Green, where once there was a large camp housing workers on the Settle-Carlisle railway. The famous Ribblehead viaduct carries the railway across the dale.**

WALK 22: Fountains Fell

Summer cloud rests on the smooth slopes of Fountains fell.

Map: Yorkshire Dales Southern Area, 1:25,000.
Start: On Silverdale Road (Stainforth–Halton Gill) just east of the gate MR842715. Huge amount of parking space on verges.
Distance: 10 miles.
Time: 5 hours.
What's it Like?: A moorland fell walk of the bracing sort, simple in concept and execution. Where it uses the Pennine Way the paths are easy to follow but sometimes boggy; where it doesn't, the paths are non-existent. Fairly strenuous, and the culminating road-walk can be exhausting on a hot day.
Shorter Alternatives: 1) Ascent of Fountains Fell from Rainscar and descent as described in text, (3^1/2 miles). Steep ascent and even steeper descent. Say, 2hrs; 2) If you can get someone to drop you off and pick you up later then it is more elegant to reverse the route, starting at the finger post at the Langcliffe road junction MR856672 (very restricted parking— not recommended to park here). The first part then becomes an interesting map-reading exercise. Also, it is more strenuous this way round! 4hrs.
Bad Weather Alternative: Retreat to Settle: Museum of North Craven Life, indoor swimming pool, lots of cafés.

A Circular Tour of a Fine Mountain

Fountains Fell is a great flat cap of gritstone moorland occupying the dead ground between the exotic limestone of Malham to the south-east, and the proud nose of Pen-y-ghent to the north-west. It is a long ridge of a mountain, incredibly rough on top where there are no paths to speak of. Access is restricted more or less to the actual summit which lies very near the Pennine Way.

What follows is a description of the classic circular tour of Fountains Fell, but a fractured description because the final part of the circuit, a cart track from Rough Close to Rainscar, is not a right of way and has been closed to walkers. Why it should be closed is beyond me—on such a well-made track there is no conceivable damage which walkers could do to the environment or anything else. The result of this exclusion is that the circuit can only be completed by walking the hard tarmac road back to base—3$\frac{1}{2}$ miles of it. This does not completely invalidate the walk, however, because from the road you get what are by far the best views of Pen-y-ghent you are likely to encounter.

The walk starts from the narrow road which joins Stainforth with Halton Gill. Just short of the farm at Rainscar there is a long strip of roadside grass which is used for parking; very popular it is too on a fine summer's day because the Pennine Way crosses the road at this point and can be used to climb Fountains Fell or Pen-y-ghent.

As far as Fountains Fell is concerned, I doubt whether many of the Pennine Way walkers ever follow the real route because it has the dubious distinction of running parallel with the road for about half a mile, and only a step or two from it! Moreover, the track is virtually non-existent, the going is extremely rough, and the temptation of the nearby tarmac too much altogether! It isn't worth joining the Pennine Way until it turns uphill to start the ascent in earnest, which it does at the next gate after Rainscar.

A path goes straight up the hillside by a wall until it reaches a ladder stile, beyond which is the Pennine Way. The wall continues straight up the hill, incredibly steep, but the path veers away to the left, slanting up the fellside until at last it eases and meets another wall. The climb is short and sharp and it leads straight to the top!

Well, almost. It actually leads to the remnants of some old coal mines, for incredible though it may seem, coal was actually mined up here during the last century. This puts the mines almost 150m higher than those at Tan Hill: another bleak coalmining site. What incredible fortitude the men must have needed to work in this God-forsaken spot!

The gritstone cap of Fountains Fell is about 170ft thick and contains several bands of coal, mostly only three or four inches thick, but with two seams of 2$\frac{1}{2}$ft thickness. One is about 160ft down but the other, which exists only on the highest part of the moor, is only 30ft below the surface. This upper seam was probably worked by bell pits from the 18th century when the coal would be used to calcine lime in the field kilns which were springing up everywhere at that time in response to the agricultural revolution. The deeper shafts, tapping the lower and better seam, began in 1807 to provide fuel for smelting the lead of Malham Moor and in 1810 a coke oven was built to provide coke for the calcining of Malham calamine, or zinc ore.

Fountains Fell is called after the abbey which owned it, but there seems to be nothing to suggest the monks ever mined the coal there. To them Fountains Fell was a vast and profitable sheep run.

The surface peat of the moor is incredibly fissured with natural trenches and pot holes, so that it looks like the Somme battlefield. With

Fountains Fell.

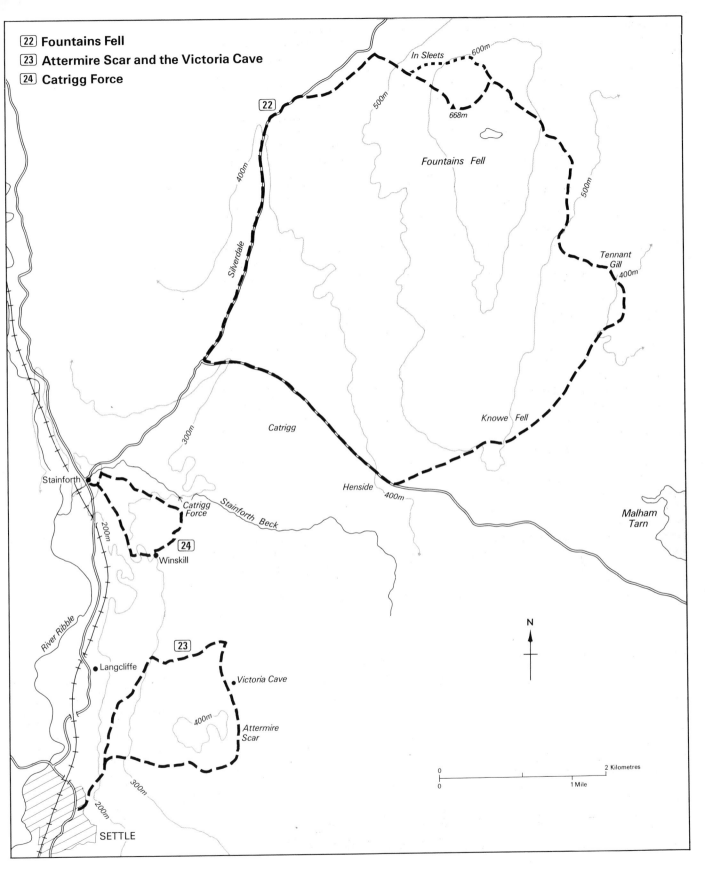

22 **Fountains Fell**
23 **Attermire Scar and the Victoria Cave**
24 **Catrigg Force**

In Sleets

600m

500m

668m

Fountains Fell

500m

400m

Silverdale

Tennant Gill

400m

Knowe Fell

300m

Catrigg

Henside

400m

Malham Tarn

Stainforth

Catrigg Force

Stainforth Beck

200m

24

Winskill

N

River Ribble

23

Langcliffe

Victoria Cave

400m

Attermire Scar

300m

0   2 Kilometres

0   1 Mile

200m

SETTLE

luck you will catch a glimpse of Fountains Fell Tarn, though to attempt to reach it needs determination, strength and a certain bone-headedness. You will certainly see the coke oven, which is still standing, and over to the south-west, about a quarter of a mile away, a prominent cairn topped by a pole.

It dawns on you, with an awful realisation, that the distant cairn is the highest point of Fountains Fell and that to achieve the ascent you have to brave the terrible land which lies between you and it. A sort of path seems to lead that way, but it tempts only to deceive—it will leave you hanging in mid-bog, so to speak. The only sure way to reach the cairn is to follow close by the summit wall where the ground is relatively easy. There's no trig block, but the cairn is considerable (668m, 2190ft).

To continue the circuit of the fell means going back to the mines, but anyone who at this point wishes to return to the car has an interesting alternative descent. Where the wall is nearest to the summit cairn there is an ancient stile which leads over the wall to the little tarns on the far side. Going past these, and following another wall, you suddenly come to the edge of all things—it is quite dramatic the way the land falls away at your feet, revealing the ribbon of road far below and across the wide vale and shapely bulk of Pen-y-ghent. The descent needs great care—it really is very steep and the path seems to disappear—but it is shortly over and you are back on the Pennine Way path, the way you came up.

In order to continue the circuit of the mountain the Pennine Way is followed to Tennant Gill and the road beyond. It is a long, sloping descent, very boggy in parts nowadays, which was formerly the coal road from the pits to Malham. There are views across Cowside Beck to the crag-beribboned fells of Arncliffe, but the chief joy of the path is the elegance with which it sweeps down the fell, curving round hollows, taking small rises in its stride.

Eventually it reaches Tennant Gill farm and the road beyond, which is the lane from Arncliffe to Malham.

For the next leg of the journey there is no path worth speaking of and you will simply waste time trying to find one. Instead, some precise navigation is called for in order to hit off the walls exactly at the gates, or stiles. Strange though it may seem this was still part of the old coal road—at least for the first mile, after which the coal road turned sharply south for High Trenhouse and Malham Moor. Walking in the direction we are it isn't too difficult to find the stiles, but coming in the opposite direction it can be quite tricky—finding the last stile straight off certainly earns brownie points!

Once you have shaken free of the various walls the aim is to head for the slight limestone crest which limits the horizon straight in front. It turns out to be a steady climb and the crest a low line of cliffs easily scrambled up. There's a large perched boulder and a fine view south-east to Malham Tarn.

It is worth taking a compass bearing from the limestone knoll to see whether you can hit off the stile in the distant wall by the accuracy of your navigation—knowing that once you get near enough you can cheat because it's a ladder stile and you can see it! (Again, it is more difficult coming from the other direction—because you don't see it until the last moment!) Beyond the wall there is still no path, but by continuing in the same general direction, the junction of the Langcliffe road with Henside Road can be identified by the tall fingerpost. At precisely that spot there is a stile over the wall, onto the road.

As I explained at the beginning, the onward journey via Rough Close and the moorland cart track is not feasible and the only way back is to walk along Henside Road, admiring the superb view of Pen-y-ghent, to the junction at Sannat Hall Farm, then along the Silverdale Road back to the car.

Facing page: **Malham Tarn seen from the walk across Knowe Fell.**

Facing page: **Pen-y-ghent seen from Henside Road** – perhaps the best of all views of this famous fell.

WALK 23: Attermire Scar and the Victoria Cave

Map: Yorkshire Dales Southern Area, 1:25,000.
Start: In the market square of Settle MR818637. Parking available in the square or various large car parks nearby. Best avoided on Tuesdays (market day).
Distance: 4 miles.
Time: 2$^1/2$ hours.
What's it Like?: A short walk but with an initially stiff climb. It would certainly be easier the other way round, but much of the dramatic impact of Warrendale Knotts and Attermire Scar is lost. Good walks seldom come easy! Suitable for all the family—caves galore, most of them pretty safe (at least for a few feet) but very muddy. Remember: caves can be dangerous places for the inexperienced—treat all of them with cautious respect.
Shorter Alternative: Park just off the Lang-cliffe–Malham road at MR830653 at the start of the lane which leads to Jubilee Cave. Climb straight up the field (no path) to a ladder stile below the cave. After examining the cave follow the track round to Victoria Cave, then return the same way. About a mile round trip.
Bad Weather Alternatives: 1) Settle in to Settle. There's a museum and public swimming baths!; 2) Take a trip on the Settle–Carlisle line while it still exists.

The Remarkable Limestone Scars of Settle

Where the River Ribble leaves the great fells which are its source, stands the town of Settle; stone built, grey and ancient, with an attractive market square, packed with stalls every Tuesday. It is an important commercial and social centre in the life of the Dales and as every schoolboy knows, Settle is connected with Carlisle by one of the most sensational feats of

The mouth of Victoria Cave.

railway engineering the Victorians ever undertook in Britain. The fate of the railway has been in the balance for some years, but most people who live in the North feel that to close it down would be an act of unprecedented vandalism.

The railway is not the only remarkable thing about Settle. High above the town—and visible from the back road to Malham—is a line of limestone crags, formed when the Middle Craven Fault displaced the land to the south downwards by a hundred metres. Eroded by the ice age, cut by cross faults, this edge—or scar, to use the local term—is positively Dolomitic in appearance. It also has some large caves.

The chief part of the crags is called Attermire Scar and the most famous cave is the Victoria Cave, so called because it was discovered in 1838, the year of Victoria's coronation. Both can be included in a short walk from Settle.

The walk starts in the market square and climbs up the steep little tarmac road called Constitution Hill until a gravelled bridleway leads off it, up the hillside. This is still steep and when after a few minutes, a signpost points to Malham, the path it indicates is steeper still. It climbs up to a broad col where it becomes much easier. I think I'm right in saying that this is probably the steepest start to any walk in this book, though memories of a hot day toiling up Flintergill at Dent are not easily forgotten! There are splendid aerial views back over the town.

The path descends into an open combe formed by Warrendale Knotts, the most spectacular shaped part of the scars. The crags rise in splendid buttresses and pinnacles, some crowned with enormous cairns. The great black hole of Spider Cave is prominent in the first Knott, whilst ahead, the long line of Attermire Scar is marked by the vertical slot of Attermire Cave. Below the scar the flat marshy ground is evidence of the shallow lake, or mire, which gave the crag its name until it was drained in Victorian times.

The path climbs a break in the crags between Warrendale Knotts and Attermire Scar, revealing that the back of the Knotts is not nearly as exciting as the front—a bit like the Langdale Pikes in the Lakes, where what you see is all there is. The back of Warrendale Knotts is grassy and lumpy and covered with a pattern of stone walls.

But on the right hand, Attermire Scar continues as Brent Scar and Langcliffe Scar, having turned through 90 degrees. The great cave can be seen from a distance and before long the path climbs up to it.

The mouth of Victoria Cave is about 100ft wide and 32ft high and the chamber extends back into the crag about 120ft, though there are low passages, known to cavers as crawls, that extend for about 450ft. The bottom of the entrance chamber is filled with boulders, and most people will be content to view the cave from the outside, where there is a broad grassy bank formed by debris excavated from the cave. The debris explains why the cave was so long in being discovered—it was so full of rubbish that there was only the merest foxhole showing, and it took a dog to find it by accident. When the cave was excavated it yielded bones and artefacts ranging from the interglacial period of 120,000 years ago, through the Stone Age and the Romano-British period of 2000 years ago. Many of them can be seen in the Settle museum.

Beyond Victoria Cave the path continues past Wet Cave and Albert Cave until it meets a broad lane which comes up from the Langcliffe road and surprisingly seems to go nowhere in particular. Where we meet it, however, is in another rocky bower, ringed about by low scars. There are two prominent caves here, Jubilee Cave and Bat Cave. Artefacts from the former can be seen in the Settle museum.

Above the caves there is a shallow gully leading to a nick in the limestone scar and by climbing up this you get a view extending right over Silverdale to Fountains Fell and Pen-y-

Warrendale Knotts.

The Walk to Victoria Cave begins and ends along this steep path out of Settle.

ghent, and across Ribblesdale to Ingleborough.

By returning to the rocky hollow a ladder stile is found which allows you to descend to the Clay Pits Plantation, whose trees are easily seen below. There is no path to speak of but the aim is for the right hand side of the plantation where access can be gained to the Langcliffe road. Almost immediately the road is abandoned for a bridleway below the plantation and across the fields, with delightful views across to Bowland. The going is easy and before long the path joins the route of ascent at the rocky lane leading to Constitution Hill and so back to the market square.

WALK 24: Catrigg Force

Stainforth in Ribblesdale.

Map: Yorkshire Dales Western Area, 1:25,000.
Start: Car park in Stainforth village MR821673.
Distance: 2 miles.
Time: 1½ hours.
What's it Like?: A suitable post-prandial exercise for the family with some very wide views and, of course, a spectacular waterfall. Surprisingly varied for such a short walk.
Shorter Alternatives: 1) Straight up and down Goat Scar Lane to the falls. Not recommended; 2) From the car park follow the main valley road to the first turning left. Follow this narrow road to the old bridge over the Ribble, then a footpath by the riverside to Stainforth Force (15 mins). The path can be followed all the way to Settle (about 2 miles).
Bad Weather Alternatives: Settle has an indoor swimming pool and the Museum of North Craven Life.

A Remarkable Waterfall

Relatively few of the guidebooks to the Dales mention Catrigg Force, a waterfall which lies deep in the fells behind the village of Stainforth. Perhaps this is because they are sidetracked by the delightful Stainforth Force on the Ribble itself, overlooked by its beautiful old packhorse bridge and with its deep plunge pool (said to be 40ft deep!) where the kids go swimming on a hot summer's day.

Nevertheless, Catrigg falls are well known because they can be quite spectacularly impressive—a great leap of 60ft in two bounces, the roar reverberating in a narrow canyon. They can be approached direct from the village by Goat Scar Lane, which is the way most people do it, but the stony lane is a brutal

93

climb and there is a far better way.

The parking at Stainforth is amongst the best in the Dales—a huge car park lies at the very entrance to the village by the Ribblesdale road. From it our walk follows the principal village street, over the bridge across the Stainforth Beck, to the village pub. Across the road from the pub a narrow lane leads in a few feet to the edge of the village where there is a kissing gate and a sign saying Winskill. The sign points towards a wooded limestone scar flanking a gently rising pasture.

The way ahead is doubtful, especially as the path virtually disappears and you seem to be trapped in an enclosure bounded by drystone walls on two sides and crags on the other. It was old George Abraham, the mountaineer, who said that sometimes if you slapped crags in the face they retreated and lost their impregnable look, and so it is in this case. At the edge of the woods a stile gives access to a delightful rock staircase which leads gently through the trees and limestone crags to the open pastures above.

A wide panorama opens towards lower Ribblesdale, the Wenning Valley and the distant fells of Bowland in Lancashire. Once again the path vanishes but the tall ladder-stiles across the walls are easy to spot and within a few minutes they lead to Lower Winskill Farm. A lane from the farm leads on past Higher Winskill to the fields beyond.

At first there is a well-marked cart track but this soon gives up and once again it is a question of spot the stile—you might also spot a few erratics here like those at Norber (see walk 20). The land begins to dip towards the Stainforth Beck and the distant views of Fountains Fell and Pen-y-ghent are very fine.

In the bottom corner of the field there are a couple of stiles and it is towards these that we make our way. The silver ribbon of the Stainforth Beck can be seen trailing across the moor and where this disappears into a copse is where the falls lie. The first stile, on the right, gives access to a narrow path on the very brink of the force and it comes as a shock to realise what a deep gorge the water has carved for itself over the years. Sheer rock walls plunge down into a deep chasm, and through the trees the top of the waterfall can be seen as it pours over the lip and roars into the canyon.

Prudence dictates that no attempt should be made to try and see the bottom of the fall! The path becomes a ledge, only a foot or so wide at one point and leaning over is not to be encouraged. There is no guide rail, nor even a handy branch to cling on to. Daring dads should not bring their young offspring along this ledge unless they want a sudden decrease in the family allowance. Fortunately there is a slightly higher and safer path, though one which doesn't offer such a good view.

Having seen the top of the force the next move is to return to the stile and then, turning through a gate on the right, cross yet another stile which gives access to the woods around the stream. A path descends below a small crag and before long leads to the foot of the waterfall. How near you can get depends on the spate at the time!

There isn't much point in following the path through the woods below the falls because it doesn't seem to lead to anywhere. There is nothing else for it but to climb back to the stile and then follow the old stony lane, Goat Scar Lane, back to Stainforth. The lane is steep and hard on the feet, but it offers superb views of Ingleborough. It leads to the village green and the walk can be rounded off in true romantic fashion by crossing the stepping stones from the green across the Stainforth Beck, on the way back to the car.

Catrigg Force.

WALK 25: The Monk's Road

Malham Tarn and Great Close Scar; the culmination of the walk from Arncliffe.

Map: Yorkshire Dales Southern Area, 1:25,000.
Start: At The Falcon, Arncliffe, MR931718.
Distance: 10 miles for the first alternative, a little less for the others.
Time: 5 hours.
What's it Like?: A very fine walk amongst the limestone scars. Good going underfoot at all times but the first bit out of Arncliffe is very steep.
Connecting Walk: You can pick up Walk 26 at Great Close Scar and follow it round Malham Cove and Gordale Scar back to the same point, then continue this walk. To do this you need at least another 3 hours. The combined walk makes for a very full day, though not specially tiring.
Shorter Alternative: Park at Darnbrook MR898705 and follow the track over the footbridge and steeply up Cowside to join the main track near Middle House. Then by Malham Tarn House and the Pennine Way, as in the first

alternative in the text, to the road and so back to Darnbrook. About 6½ miles, just over one of which is on the road.
Bad Weather Alternative: None—tough luck.

Arncliffe to Malham along an Old Monastic Path

Littondale branches off Wharfedale rather less than a mile north of Kilnsey. It is a quiet backwater of a place with ancient hamlets like Halton Gill and Litton, and a more substantial central village at Arncliffe. With its village green and the old Falcon inn, Arncliffe is a very attractive place. The Falcon was once called 'The Leg of Mutton'—well, I suppose Falcon sounds better and anyway, the name Arncliffe means *eagle*, so there's some sort of logic in it. It was here, at Bridge House, that

Charles Kingsley set the beginning of his famous novel *The Water Babies* and Littondale is the Vendale of the book.

Joining Littondale at Arncliffe is the deep narrow valley of the Cowside Beck, extremely steep sided, especially on the south, where Yew Cogar Scar draws bands of white limestone along the dale side like layers of cream in a sponge cake. Each layer has a ledge above it and on one specially broad ledge there is a path climbing up to the moors which was used by the monks of Fountains Abbey to visit their various granges on the valuable sheep runs up there.

Malham Moor, as a glance at the map will show, is criss-crossed with roads and tracks of all sorts. Many were inaugurated by the monks (though I suspect quite a few were in existence long before the monks appeared) and were later adapted to the needs of drovers, jaggers and miners. But this one, marked on the map as Monk's Road, is only a thread of a path and makes a beautiful walk for a summer's afternoon. Or, if you are feeling fit, it can be joined to Walk 26—in which case you'll need a full day to appreciate everything.

The route starts by the side of The Falcon along an old walled lane until a signpost to Malham points through a wicket gate to the open fell. The path is clearly marked with numerous cairns. At first it climbs very steeply to its grassy ledge above the crag, then more gradually perhaps, but with a certain relentless determination. For the first three miles it hardly ever eases off—but what the heck. . . it is a path to savour gradually anyway, with endless combinations of fascinating limestone architecture made by God for Man's appreciation.

Across Cowside Beck tiny cars can be seen crawling up and down the narrow road to Darnbrook House.

By the time you reach Middle House, which was the abbey grange, you will feel that the old monks earned their crust. When I passed this way in 1988 the place was being restored by one of those nebulous employment schemes, though to what end wasn't apparent. It is a very lonely site and has its limitations even as a week-end cottage, one would have thought.

A little further and the path dips steeply downhill to Middle House Farm, built in the last century and still very active. Great Close Hill rises steeply on the right, hiding the Tarn, but most of Malham Moor seems to roll away before your feet for ever. It is easy to pick out Gordale Scar, even three miles away.

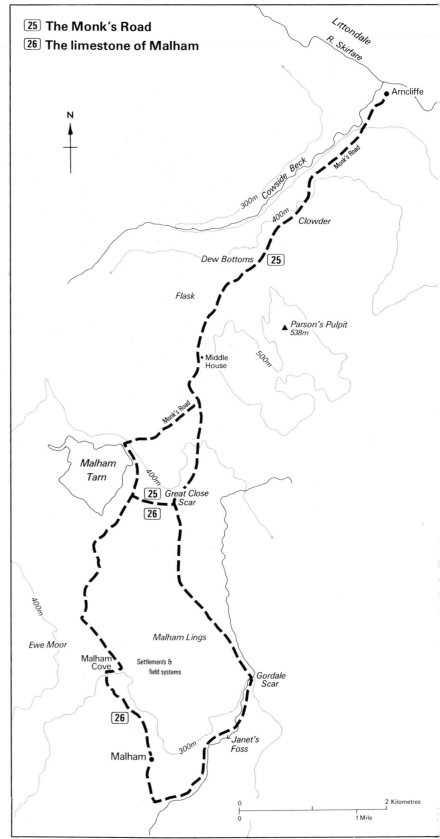

25 **The Monk's Road**
26 **The limestone of Malham**

Above: **The Monk's Road rises steeply out of Arncliffe village.**

Overleaf: **Cowside Beck and Yew Cogar Scar: the route follows limestone ledges above the scar.**

paths available.

The Tarn comes as a revelation if you haven't seen it before—it is so much bigger than one expects; a sombre place too, with a strange feeling of loneliness. It covers 153 acres and is 14 feet deep. On the northern shore there is a prominent boathouse to be seen (one of a pair) backed by dense woods, and it is towards these that we direct our steps. A major decision has to be made—and soon!

The fact is, there are three alternative ways back to Arncliffe and since each has its merits you pays your money and takes your choice. Here they are.

The broad path by the side of the Tarn is part of the Pennine Way. It leads into the woods, cool and quiet on a hot summer's day, and to Malham Tarn House which is a field study centre. Passing behind the house (a building utterly devoid of architectural merit) it continues to a point where a signpost directs the Pennine Wayfarer into a field and on to a path which will take him below the West End limestone scars to the tarmac road to Darnbrook. From the Tarn, this is about a mile and a half, and the only way back to Arncliffe is along the tarmac road, dipping deep and steep into Darnbrook where Darnbrook House is another old grange of Fountains Abbey. Although it is more than three miles perhaps this is not as bad as it seems. You can walk off the road for much of the time and the views across Cowside Beck to Yew Cogar are certainly worth seeing.

But if the thought of all that road tramping puts you off then where the road by the Tarn meets the woods, turn right and climb the gentle grass slopes to the saddle above and decend even gentler slopes back to Middle House Farm. A purist will no doubt gain smug satisfaction from knowing this completes the Monk's Road and now the way back lies in a return to Middle House and a diversion just beyond it, well seen, which leads as straight as an arrow steeply down into Cowside Beck at the junction with Darnbrook. This is a flamboyant descent, with some unusual views of the beck in its latter stages—and a disconcerting view of Nab End, which has to be climbed by the zig-zag road! The final descent to Arncliffe is still along the road, but this time for some two miles only.

And finally, of course, you can always go back the way you came, having crossed the saddle to reach Middle House Farm. Why not? The views are stunning—and the walking's a lot easier this way round!

The true line of the Monk's Road lies over the low saddle to the north of Great Close Hill and so to Malham Tarn and this is certainly an option which is open to the walker. It also saves a mile, but I think it is a mile well travelled, even though the first half is along a disintegrating tarmac road to Great Close Plantation. From the Plantation an old track travels to the Tarn beneath Great Close Scar, an attractive limestone outcrop sometimes used by rock climbers. On a busy weekend the wide view over Malham Moor will show an amazing pattern of walkers criss-crossing in every which way as they follow the numerous

WALK 26: The Limestone of Malham

Malham.

Map: Yorkshire Dales Southern Area, 1:25,000.
Start: Car park in village at MR900628.
Distance: 6½ miles.
Time: Take at least 3 hours and preferably longer.
What's it Like?: An interesting excursion in a fascinating landscape full of grand gestures. A bit of scrambling required in Gordale, otherwise the going is easy.
Shorter Alternatives: A return to Malham can be made from each feature of the walk, thus: from Janet's Foss and the *mauvais pas* of Gordale Scar, along Gordale Lane (1hr); from above Gordale by Malham Rakes lane (1½hrs). The Cove and Dry Valley direct from Malham and back (1hr). The network of paths and roads makes numerous variations possible. Walkers should keep strictly to the paths in this area; the sheer pressure of visitors makes the landowners touchy.

Bad Weather Alternative: Settle is the nearest bolt-hole. It has an indoor swimming pool and the Museum of North Craven Life.

Breathtaking Scenery in a Geological Wonderland

Is there any place in England where the scenery is more astonishing than at Malham? No matter how often you see it it never palls for there is always some extra extravagance in the towering rocks that you had not noticed before. 'The sight of the Cove always surprises and the sight of Gordale always astounds,' was how a recent writer put it. An earlier chronicler said, 'The imagination can scarcely figure any form or scale of rock within the bounds of probability that shall go beyond it.' Small wonder then that the great and good have been

99

frequent visitors since the dawn of tourism, followed in more recent years by earnest bands of schoolchildren clutching pad and pencil with which to record the mysteries of limestone, not to mention the casual tourist by the thousand. Whoever invented the term 'honeypot site' must have had Malham in mind.

So the place is popular and likely to be crowded, but this does not invalidate it. The experience of Malham transcends all such petty irritations.

There are three principal features to see: the Cove, Gordale Scar and Malham Tarn. There are also a number of secondary features worth including in a walk: Janet's Foss, Great Close Scar, the Dry Valley and the pavement on top of the Cove. The following walk embraces all these and though it is only 6½ miles it is likely to take longer to complete than might normally be the case for this distance. In fact it is not so much a walk; more an exploration. At one point, in Gordale, it even involves a bit of scrambling where you must trust your hands as well as your feet.

The walk starts from the car park at the southern edge of the village. Almost opposite there is a footbridge across the Malham Beck from where a path (actually the Pennine Way) can be followed to the right. Before long Mires Barn appears and at this point a left turn is made to follow a good path for a mile to Janet's Foss, a pretty waterfall overlooking a pool and cave where a water sprite, Jennet, was reputed to live. On a hot day you can sometimes still see water sprites here!

Janet's Foss is adjacent to a narrow tarmac road called Gordale Lane and by continuing the walk up this for a short distance the signpost for Gordale Scar is seen. A path leads directly into the impressive chasm. Overhanging walls of limestone rear up for 150 feet. On them can sometimes be seen bits of coloured tape left behind by rock climbers, for incredible as it may seem to the layman, these stupendous walls have been climbed.

The rocks funnel in until the gorge is no more than a mere slit, blocked by a tumbled boulder down which a minor waterfall

Gordale Scar is one of the most impressive scenic experiences in England. (Photo: Duncan Unsworth.)

splashes. If the water is very high and coming down in force, or the boulder iced up on a cold winter's day, then the walk might end right here, for this is the *mauvais pas*. This is the place where the walker must literally take his life in his hands—or so it seems, though the scramble up the boulder is really not difficult and quite short. Nevertheless there is a *frisson*, because it is the key to a secret place, the inner sanctum of the gorge. The way is rough and the surroundings are wild, like something out of *Lord of the Rings*. A waterfall splashes from a hole high in the rocks.

As the gorge turns a corner the path climbs out of it onto the fellside above which is all hummocks and dry valleys and little limestone scars. There seems a plethora of paths here, but by heading north you will eventually fetch up at an attractively sculpted limestone crag called Great Close Scar. A bridleway runs below the rocks and leads to the shore of the Tarn.

At 375m (1226ft), Malham Tarn is the highest limestone lake in the country, a condition which leads to some interesting flora. It owes its existence to an upthrust of slates, impervious to water and further sealed by glacial clays from the moraines of the Ice Age glacier which scooped it out, though it was enlarged to its present size in 1780 when Lord Ribblesdale dammed the outflow and raised the water level. It covers 153 acres and is 14 feet deep.

At the northern end of the lake is Tarn House surrounded by woods; once a shooting lodge but a field study centre since 1948. It would be hard to envisage a better site, for besides the rocks and flora the tarn is home to many birds.

Nevertheless, Malham Tarn is a melancholy sort of place. The lake needs the backing of great mountains to give it life, and this it does not have.

A path (the Pennine Way again) runs south and one of many branches leads to the Tarn's outflow and an area known as Water Sinks because that is just what the stream does—vanish underground. Logic dictates that the stream should reappear at the foot of the Cove, because it is in direct line, but logic is wrong in this case—the stream reappears below Malham village. Nevertheless it is easy to follow the surface line of the stream into the beautiful Dry Valley which ends at the limestone pavement on top of the Cove.

The view is startling, original. The flat pavement, cracked and fissured into clints and grikes spreads forward to a sudden sharp edge beyond which there is only space and a distant landscape. A little care is needed, especially in wet weather, for the limestone can be slippery and it is easy to twist a leg in one of the cracks. Going too near the edge is not advisable; the drop is sheer for almost 300ft.

Since the school parties started coming to Malham in numbers, the top of the Cove has become the archetypal limestone pavement example. I wonder how many exam papers it has appeared in? I wonder if the children (or teachers) know there are other and better examples elsewhere?

But such philosophical considerations need not detain us. By going to the right-hand side of the pavement (looking out) we come across a rather well-made path (it's the Pennine Way again, folks!) which leads easily down the steep slopes to the foot of the rocks.

The impact of this crag on the senses is truly awesome. It soars up like some gigantic petrified manta ray with a great brooding, hooded body and two fins, one on either side. In ancient time water came down the Dry Valley and poured over the lip in what must have been a truly spectacular sight. Even as late as 1850 the waterfall sometimes appeared in periods of heavy rain, but there's no record of it in modern times.

You can walk up to the wall and watch the little stream bubbling out at the base, and wonder how such a noble parent can sire such a miserable offspring. Looking up you may see the tell-tale marks of climbers, as you did in Gordale, and wonder again at the skill and nerve of the modern crag-rat.

The show is over; as grand a display of geological pyrotechnics as you are likely to see in Britain. From the Cove all paths lead to the village and, in less than a mile, the car.

Malham Tarn.

Malham Cove – a waterfall once poured over the lip.

WALK 27: Bolton Abbey to Barden Bridge

Bolton Priory and the stepping stones across the Wharfe.

Map: Yorkshire Dales Southern Area, 1:25,000. A map is useful though not essential for this walk.

Start: Bolton Abbey car park MR071539 (pay). Because it is a circular walk it could be started from the Barden Bridge car park or the Pavilion car park instead.

Distance: 7 miles.

Time: 3½ hours.

What's it Like?: A riverside walk of great charm if done out of season. Not a place for anyone who likes solitude, though in between the high points such as the Strid, Pavilion, Priory and Barden Bridge you probably won't meet all that many people. Can be walked in trainers.

Shorter Alternatives: Park at the Pavilion (MR077552) and using the bridge there walk either to the Priory and back, or Barden Bridge and back. About an hour and 2½ hours re-

spectively, including time to look at the buildings.

Bad Weather Alternative: There's probably something to be said for doing this walk in the rain! Plenty of shelter, one way and another—the church, the Pavilion, Yorkshire Crafts etc.

Along the Banks of the Wharfe

Between Barden Bridge and Bolton Abbey the River Wharfe flows through a largely wooded dale owned by the Duke of Devonshire who administers it through a Trust called the Chatsworth Settlement—Chatsworth being the Duke's home in the Peak District. It is administered extremely efficiently and is a prime tourist attraction so that on a warm weekend in summer or a Bank Holiday you will probably see as many people here as in the

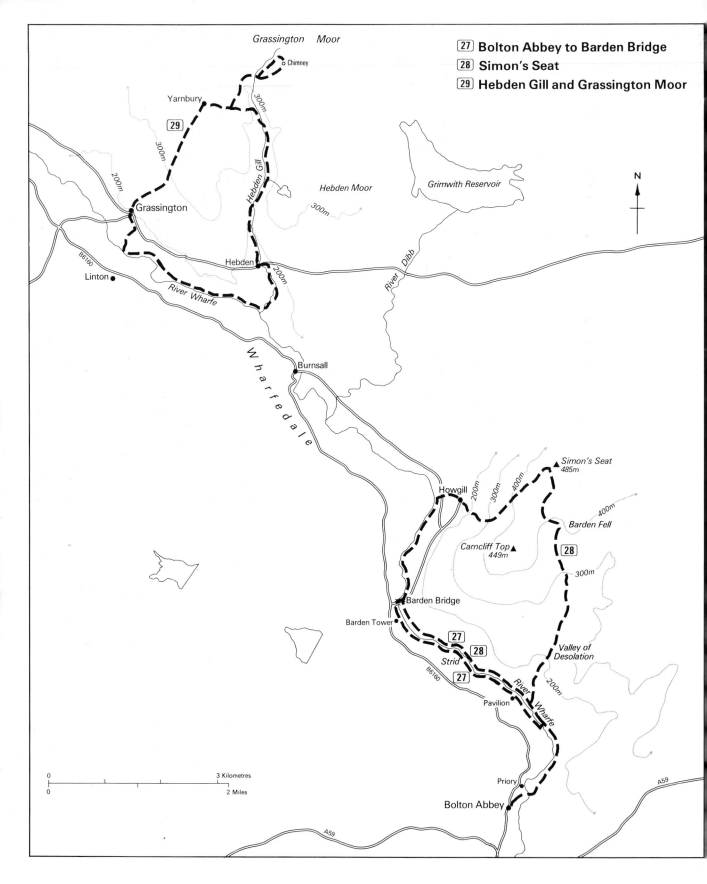

The Strid.

The path leads to a wooden bridge across the river alongside which a row of stepping stones of much older foundation can be seen and from the opposite side a newly restored path climbs steeply up a flank of the valley. From here you get the best of all views of Bolton Priory, in its idyllic setting, including the great ruined east window. The curve of the river, the stepping stones, make for a scene of rare beauty.

Bolton Priory was founded in 1154 by Augustinian canons (known as Black Friars because they wore black habits and not, as a schoolboy once wrote, because of their dirty habits!). It became a wealthy establishment which, in its heyday, had up to twenty canons, several lay brethren, and employed 200 people. It was suppressed in 1539; three years after the Act of Dissolution. The Priory had always been the village church which is why the King allowed a portion to remain intact—it is still a rather grand church for such a small village.

After a stiff climb the path levels out high above the Wharfe and enters a thick wood. There are glimpses of the river from time to time but mostly the enjoyment—in spring and summer, anyway—comes from the varied carpet of flowers growing beneath the trees.

Where Pickles Beck trickles down off the moors the path meets the narrow road which runs along this side of the dale. The road crosses the beck by a ford and you need to take care that you don't tackle this at the same time as a passing car, for though the ford is wide enough it is extremely slippery and any distraction will certainly cause a tumble and wetting. The path at once leaves the road again beyond the ford and goes down to the river bank which it follows through a meadow to the wooden bridge at the Cavendish Pavilion.

This is the least inspiring part of the walk. The opposite bank is one enormous car park and what with the Pavilion offering teas and ices, nature trails and toilet facilities, the river and its banks are alive with humanity on any fine weekend.

Naturally, we press on sternly, resisting the temptations of the flesh. The path continues on the same side of the river as before but now it becomes less well-made, though still perfectly distinguishable. There's an island in the river about here, just visible through the dense foliage. Once again the path meets the road for a yard or two and then plunges down through the woods in one of the most exciting parts of the walk. At times it follows rock ledges by the very edge of the river like a minor version of

rest of the Dales put together! At the Cavendish Pavilion and Barden Bridge car parks the vehicles stand rank upon rank by the river's edge while their owners sun themselves on the grass, swim in the river or play volley ball with the kids. It is not a pretty sight. This is the Blackpool of the Dales.

So timing is crucial on this walk. If it has to be summer, choose midweek, but better still choose autumn or winter when the river is at its most magical. For let there be no misunderstanding—take away the crowds and the walk is a delight.

The walk begins at the Hole in the Wall at Bolton Abbey, which is actually the name of a village and not the impressive ruin by the river's edge—that is Bolton Priory. The Hole in the Wall is exactly what it says, and through the hole a set of steps leads down to the riverside meadows. The Priory is on the left—a curious hybrid of a ruin insofar as half of it isn't ruined at all, being still used as the parish church. In front of it is the schoolhouse built by Robert Boyle, often called 'the father of chemistry' and the discoverer of Boyle's Law.

Above: **Barden Tower, home of the Shepherd Lord.**

Facing page: **Barden Bridge.**

several others have had the misfortune to fall in through trying to get too close. The rocks can be slippery.

The turbulent nature of the Wharfe continues with another less impressive narrowing called the High Strid a few yards upstream, but soon it returns to its normal complacent self. The path emerges from the woods at a curious bridge, decorated with crenellated turrets in the best Victorian folly style. Was it built to carry waterpipes over the river? It seems unpardonable extravagance just to be a footbridge.

A walk through the riverside meadows brings Barden Bridge in view. It is one of the oldest and most attractive of the Wharfe's bridges; three segmental arches of stone spanning 55 yards in length but only ten feet wide between parapets. It carries the road to Appletreewick across the river and pedestrians can shelter from the traffic in the recesses of the big cutwaters.

The return leg of this walk is along the opposite bank of the river, but before we do that it is worth following the road uphill (and steep it is, too!) to Barden Tower, one of the most romantic of Lady Anne Clifford's castles.

The tall, square tower of Barden is reminiscent of a Border peel. Originally it was a hunting lodge, one of eight such in the wide forests of Barden, though the most important one because it was the administrative centre where the Swainmote Court was held and forest laws executed. In 1310 it came into the hands of the Cliffords, along with Skipton Castle, their principal residence.

None of the Cliffords lived at Barden regularly until 1485, when Henry Clifford, known as The Shepherd Lord, made his home there. Henry's father—Blackfaced Clifford, child murderer and a pretty bad lot—had been attainted for backing the wrong side in the Wars of the Roses and his mother had sent her two sons into hiding, fearing for their lives. One died in the Netherlands but Henry, sent to live with shepherds in Threlkeld, Cumberland, survived to inherit his fortune after Bosworth when Dick Plantagenet was killed and Henry VII became king.

Interested in astronomy and alchemy, Henry preferred the isolation of Barden to Skipton, though he was not a recluse. By all accounts Barden was a lively place during his time. He was married twice, with several sons and daughters, and led his own troops at Flodden in 1513.

It was Henry who added the chapel which is

the famous Nunnery Walks on the River Eden in Cumbria and then it leads on to broad flat slabs which come together and squeeze the river into a narrow channel through which the water rushes like a miniature High Force. This is the Strid, where the Boy of Egremont, son of Alice de Romilly of Skipton Castle, is said to have met his death in the 12th century as he tried to jump across whilst chasing deer. This may be simply legend, but it is a fact that

The Priory and the stepping stones over the Wharfe at Bolton Abbey. (Photo: F. Leonard Jackson.)

now the farmhouse serving teas and ices. An ancestor of the family who lives there, fought with Henry at Flodden.

When Henry died in 1523 the Tower declined to temporary use again. It fell into disrepair and was only put into order by the indefatigable Lady Anne Clifford in the mid-17th century, as a memorial stone set into the south wall testifies to this day. Strictly speaking, Barden Tower did not actually belong to Anne, but a small detail like that was unlikely to deter her and nobody was going to argue. Certainly not Lady Elizabeth Clifford to whom it rightfully belonged. She was no match for the formidable grand dame of the Clifford clan! She got her property back on Anne's death in 1676.

After refreshments at the Tower we must retrace our steps down the hill to the bridge where a squeeze stile gives access to the riverside path. The return journey is similar in many respects to the outward one although the views might be thought rather finer. The paths are good though more numerous than on the opposite bank because of the various nature trails. Eventually they lead to the Cavendish Pavilion where there is a kiosk by the gate—and a possible entry fee. If it is late in the day, however, you are not likely to be charged.

Beyond the Pavilion that side of the river is boring so it is preferable to cross the footbridge and return by the early part of the outward route. There is a temptation to stay low, by the river, the whole way, but it should be resisted—there is no way through after Pickles Beck. Better to climb up to the road then follow the maintained path back to the Stepping Stones and the Priory.

WALK 28: Simon's Seat

Looking up Wharfedale from
Barden Fell; one of the finest
views in the Dales.

Map: Yorkshire Dales Southern Area, 1:25,000.
Start: Waterfall Cottage (not named on map)
MR076554. Room for a few cars near here but
more certain parking at Pavilion Car Park (pay).
Distance: 8 miles (Pavilion Car Park).
Time: 5 hours.
What's it Like?: A fine little mountain ascent,
very varied, with a stunning view from the top.
Takes about 1½hrs to reach the summit. Good
paths throughout.
Connections with other Walks: At Barden
Bridge the walk follows the paths used in Walk
27.
Shorter Alternatives: 1) Return by same
route as ascent (3hrs); 2) From Howgill (limited
parking at Lane junction) follow Howgill Lane
until near Dalehead Farm. A path leaves the
Lane and winds up through the woods, then
climbs up steep open moor to the summit rocks.
A direct and dramatic approach. Return to

Howgill by route described in text (2hrs).
Bad Weather Alternatives: Wharfedale is full
of tourist attractions for those with a car—
Barden Tower (good afternoon teas),
Grassington (where every other building is a
restaurant of one sort or another). Many more.

The Valley of Desolation to Barden Fell

The ascent of Simon's Seat is a proper little
mountain climb which manages to encapsulate
all that is best in Dales' walking. Everything
for which the Dales are famous—waterfalls,
wild moors, gritstone crags, river paths and
even green roads are represented to some
degree. It also has what is probably the finest
view in Wharfedale

The walk begins up the Posforth Gill which

splashes down the moors into the River Wharfe a few hundred yards upstream from the Pavilion, though on the other bank. The Pavilion may be the best place to park—especially as nowadays there are warnings about cars being left unattended in the smaller parking spaces—though there's room for half a dozen cars near the gate where the walk commences. From the Pavilion simply cross the footbridge over the river and walk up the road to the house called Waterfall Cottage which is the old Deer Park Lodge, where the gate is marked by a large and fading access map.

A path leads through pleasant parkland once inhabited by deer. A small hill up ahead looks interesting and the path climbs towards it in a vague sort of way, but the wanderer is distracted by the increasing noise of the Posforth beck. In a typically wet summer it positively roars, as a guide once informed some less-than-interested Victorian visitors.

'I can't hear it', protested one of the men.

'You will, sir,' said the guide blandly, 'as soon as the ladies stop talkin'.'

The main path goes uphill, but remembering General Stonewall Jackson's admirable advice on tactics (follow the sound of the gunfire) take the minor path down to the roaring beck. The water flows through a wooded glade and a good path leads upstream through the trees to the superb Posforth Gill waterfall.

Twin spouts pour over a lip of rock into a shallow pool which forms the bottom of a green bower. The slopes rise steeply all round, cloaked with shrubs and trees. Idyllic is the word which springs to mind; a secret garden known only to wanderers like yourself.

In a dry season it is possible to cross the stream and climb up the other bank until it meets Waterfall Bridge, but when the stream is full you stand a good chance of a wetting. Then the only recourse is to retreat and join the main path up the hill more or less where you left it. This is no bad thing anyway because there are lovely glimpses of the falls and the first sight of the bridge and Valley of Desolation are quite superb.

The path goes over the little bridge and climbs the opposite bank above a small, narrow valley so full of lush vegetation that the gill cannot be seen. It is as pretty a little dell as you are likely to find anywhere, so why is it called the Valley of Desolation? Was it the scene of some terrible massacre? Did the Black Death strike out an ancient hamlet? Alas, history reveals nothing so dramatic. The

boring truth is that about 150 years ago a great storm flattened the trees, and hence the name.

Once it has climbed out of the valley the path joins a bridleway which is an access route for shooting parties. The hill belongs to the Devonshire estates and it is a well-kept grouse moor where, until recent times, you needed a permit to walk. The bridleway leads through some tall pines, planted in 1832 according to a metal plaque—I wonder if they were planted to replace those lost in the storm which wrecked

Posforth Falls near the start of the walk up Simon's Seat.

the Valley of Desolation, or whether it is just a coincidence that the two things should happen about the same time?

Before long the bridleway breaks free of the trees and there is a sudden change to open moorland, which rolls away on either hand. Up ahead there is a deep and narrow clough with the path crawling up the side of it towards the distant horizon, and made an unsightly white by the use of limestone chippings to repair it. Limestone chippings do not sit well on a gritstone moor!

There commences at this point the only arduous part of the whole climb. The track slogs up the side of the Agill beck remorselessly until at Great Agill Head it slackens off. Massive clumps of rock appear, like miniature Dolomites but made of gritstone; tors of the finest quality. The path heads towards the highest of these and with a bit of a scramble reaches the trig block.

This rocky knoll is Simon's Seat. Each of the

surrounding tors has a name too—the Hen Stones, Lord's Seat and so on—brought about by the striking formations which erosion has given them. In places they are quite high—even on the approach side, across the moor, they must be twenty or thirty feet, and on the northern side, overlooking Skyreholme, Simon's Seat is twice that. There are rock climbs here though the place has never been popular with climbers—too far for the modern crag-rat to walk. On some of the shorter faces, youngsters can sometimes be seen, under instruction.

Reaching the top of Simon's Seat is quite a revelation. There opens up, quite suddenly, a tremendous vista over upper Wharfedale, flanked on the one hand by the Rylstone moors and on the other by the deep gash of Troller's Gill. Skyreholme and Appletreewick look like Toytown villages and you seem to be hovering over them because the land below falls away with dramatic suddeness.

From the summit rocks a peaty path leads along the edge of the moor until it meets at a gate with a bridlepath coming up from Howgill. The path descends rapidly towards the valley crossing Howgill Lane, an old green road, until it meets the bridge where the narrow surfaced road from Barden Bridge to Appletreewick crosses the Fir Beck. Here a path leads down to the river bank which can be followed to Barden Bridge. At first this is not very interesting because the trees keep the path away from the river but it soon improves and the middle stretch is very lovely, with the Wharfe at its best.

At Barden Bridge there is a choice of route along either bank of the river (see Walk 27) back to the Pavilion car park. Those in a hurry will choose the right-hand bank, but with time to spare the left-hand bank is a shade more adventurous.

WALK 29: Hebden Gill and Grassington Moor

Linton church served Linton, Grassington and Hebden in the old days. The stepping stones across the Wharfe were to give the people of Hebden direct access to the church.

Map: Yorkshire Dales Southern Area, 1:25,000.
Start: The National Park car park in Hebden Road, Grassington (pay), MR003637. This is almost opposite the bus station.
Distance: 8½ miles.
Time: 4hrs—or more, depending on your interest in the mining remains.
What's it Like?: A very varied walk, full of interest throughout. Very good paths for the most part and not strenuous, though you will know you've been for a walk and the moor can be bitterly cold at times. The area round Yarnbury has the most extensive mining remains in the Dales, and the village of Grassington is a great tourist attraction in its own right.
Shorter Alternatives: 1) From Hebden return directly to Grassington by High Lane (5 miles); 2) As in the text but omit the mines by returning directly to Grassington via Tinker's Lane from Hebden Gill (6½miles); 3) Drive to Yarnbury and follow the mining trail. A couple of miles at most, but needs more time than you might think.
Bad Weather Alternatives: 1) There is much of interest in Grassington including a folk museum. Often exhibitions etc at the Town Hall; 2) Stump Cross Caverns, a show cave, is some 5½ miles along the Pateley Bridge road, B6265.
Warning: All mining remains hold danger for the unwary. This is specially so on the Grassington moor where there are dangerous shafts. These may not be particularly obvious—indeed, they may appear to be filled, when in fact they have only been capped. Areas of particular danger are displayed on prominent boards at Yarnbury and elsewhere. If you stick to the proper paths you will be quite safe. When walking the underground flues remember they are 200 years old and so walk at the side of them not on top! Never try to enter adits or levels.

Wharfedale's Industrial Past

Everyone who knows the Yorkshire Dales has his or her own favourite dale, but for sheer variety Wharfedale is hard to beat. This dale has everything from high gritstone moors like Buckden Pike and Barden Fell, to spectacular limestone formations like Kilnsey Crag with its great overhang and the savage little gorge of Troller's Gill. The river, too, is exceptionally fine with wonderful old bridges and villages which look as though they were designed for postcards. There is industry too, and though the mills of yesterday are mostly gone or converted into bijou residences, there is still quarrying to blot the landscape. Above all, in this respect, there are the remains of the lead mining which so dominated the middle valley around Grassington in the 18th and 19th centuries.

The Grassington field was one of two mining fields in the Dales, the other being Swaledale. A *field* is where numerous lead veins, and therefore numerous mines, are gathered close together. The Grassington field laps over into Nidderdale, just as the Swaledale field laps over into Arkengarthdale and Wensleydale—all the other scattered mines are what Arthur Raistrick, the great authority on mining in the Pennines, calls fringe deposits.

The walk about to be described combines much that is quintessential about Wharfedale; it marries the river and the moor or as some might have it, beauty and the beast.

It starts from the National Park car park in Hebden Road where, from the bottom corner, an ancient narrow ginnel known as the Snake Walk leads down to the river. The lane is also known as the Flags, and traces of flags can still be seen in places. It leads directly to the riverside path by the Linton Falls and a girder bridge across to Linton. Called the Tin Bridge locally, it replaces an earlier one swept away by floods at the turn of the century. In its turn, the present bridge is closed as being unsafe (1988), but no doubt it will be repaired because there has been a crossing of the Wharfe here for centuries.

The bridge was part of the network of paths which led to Linton church, for the parish of Linton included Grassington, Threshfield and Hebden in the old days. The church is an ancient foundation with a curious overhanging bell turret and can be well seen across the river from our present paths, beyond the cluster of houses known as Botany—a name indicating a mill colony, which is what it once was. Lower down stream, at a bend in the river there are some stepping stones which was the way from Hebden to the church—but the river, is wide at this point and flows strongly. When the water is high the stones scarcely show and many a worshipper must have offered up prayers with more than usual fervour!

The path cuts across a grassy peninsula to meet the river bank again under the shade of some superb horse chestnut trees. On the left

Below left: **Hebden**.

Below right: **The underground flue and its chimney on Grassington moor, built to serve the Duke's new smelter of 1793**.

the ground rises steeply and there is no escape until a suspension bridge appears, where Hebden Beck joins the river. A path leads up by the Hebden Beck and through the village to the main Grassington to Pateley Bridge road.

From the road bridge over the beck the old bridge can be seen, made obsolete when the road was realigned during turnpiking early in the 19th century. Our way in fact leads past this bridge along a narrow surfaced road on the west bank of the stream for about half a mile to Hole Bottom, perhaps better known as Jerry and Ben Cottage. Just before this it is possible to go down to the stream to see Scala Force, an attractive waterfall, and from the cottage itself the view upstream of the narrow valley with its fringe of gritstone crags is most romantic.

Beyond Hole Bottom the surfaced road becomes a rough path known as Limekiln Lane, which we can follow all the way to Yarnbury on Grassington moor. It leads up the valley through various mining remains into a landscape which grows increasingly barren.

The portals of various mining levels can be seen, including the important Duke's level, driven from Hebden Gill below the main Grassington veins in order to drain them. It was started in 1796 and the original idea was to make it an underground canal, like the Duke of Bridgewater had for his coal mines at Worsley in Lancashire. However, this grandiose scheme was abandoned after a few years and a narrower, less ambitious tunnel continued. Even so, it took 28 years to complete and cost the Duke £33,000. Just to give some idea of what this means, the distance from the portal in Hebden Gill to the smelt mill on the moor, which it takes you a half hour or so to walk, took 24 years of hard tunnelling!

Where the gill starts to open out there are old slag heaps through which the path winds, climbing steeply to the moor. In the distance across the gill can be seen a tall chimney and two areas of extensive ruins. Slag heaps and dereliction lie all round and it is obvious that you are standing amongst the decaying skeletons of a once great industry.

It is hard to believe that the peaceful and attractive Hebden Gill was once the scene of busy lead mining industry.

Lead mining was the life-blood of Grassington during the 18th and 19th centuries, especially at the Duke of Devonshire's mines which are centred on Yarnbury. He it was who had the Duke's Level driven to drain the mines and paradoxically he also has a long and expensive channel dug to *bring* water to the mines—but surface water with which to drive the many water wheels. Dams were created to keep the channel flowing, crushing mills were installed to grind the ore and, of course, there was a smelt mill, the ruins of which can still be seen, just across Hebden Gill.

Most of these features were connected by a lane known as the Duke's New Road (to distinguish it from the adjacent Old Moor Lane) and our path turns on to this. It leads across an old dam on Hebden Gill and to the remains of the Cupola Mill, rebuilt in 1793 with two reverbatory furnaces which were much more efficient than the old ore hearths. 300 tons of lead a year was produced.

Such furnaces needed fierce fires, and that resulted in the long flues and tall chimneys seen on the moor above the mill. Originally there were two chimneys. Valuable lead condensed on the flues and in the Stokoe condensers, the ruins of which can be seen if you follow the flue up to the chimney from the mill. The lead and soot was washed out from time to time into settling tanks. Branch flues can be seen, and the whole business was nothing if not ingenious.

From the chimney it is easy to cross the short stretch of moor to the second group of ruins. This was the site of the crushing mill where the ore was prepared for smelting but it bears little relation today to what it was like in the Duke's time because it was adapted by a chemical company in the 1950s for the working of fluorspar from the spoil heaps. Before that however, it was badly damaged by the army who used the moor as a gunnery range during the last world war.

A lead mining 'trail' has been established on the moor round Yarnbury, so that each point of interest is numbered and explained on a display board. Unfortunately there is no leaflet to go with the trail, which seems to largely invalidate the exercise.

From the site of the High Grinding Mill our way follows the Duke's Road back across the moor to Yarnbury; attractive dwellings in what was once the administrative buildings of the mines. From here Moor Lane, surfaced but with wide grassy edges, leads directly down into Grassington. This was the way the miners came home and when they reached the prominent rise, just before the village, they could smell their dinners cooking—which is why for many years the place was called Hungry Laugh Hill.

About the village itself little need be said because it has all been said before. As one writer put it: Grassington is everybody's favourite Dale village. It is the Clovelly, the Grasmere, the Bourton of the Dales and if it is popular, then thank goodness, at least it hasn't been spoilt.

WALK 30: Old Cote Moor and the Horse Head Pass

Map: Yorkshire Dales Central Area, 1:25,000.
Start: Buckton car park, MR942774.
Distance: 13 miles.
Time: 6½ hours.
What's it Like?: This walk embodies much that is finest in Dales walking—the crossing of the Horse Head Pass and the limestone shelf from Yockenthwaite to Cray being particularly good. There are two major ascents involved—1200ft from Buckden to Old Cote Moor and about 1000ft from Halton Gill to Horse Head Gate. The minor ascents at Yockenthwaite and Cray can be little knee bucklers near the end of a fairly long, hard day!
Shorter Alternative: From Buckden follow the Dales Way along the river via Hubberholme to Yockenthwaite then return as described in the text (7 miles).
Bad Weather Alternative: Drive over the pass to Aysgarth to see the falls, and carriage mu-seum. Castle Bolton, the ancient home of the Scropes, and Middleham Castle, favourite residence of Richard III are not far away and worth seeing.

From Buckden to Litton and Back

Buckden is the last village of any size up Wharfedale. On the east it is dominated by the large bulk of Buckden Pike (see Walk 32) while to the west there is a long but lower moor known as Old Cote, after a house of the same name in Littondale, the valley on the other side of the moor. A cote was an abbey grange farm. It has long been a favourite pastime amongst walkers to stay in one valley and walk over the moor to sample the beer in the next, and it doesn't matter which way round because the

From the limestone scars at the head of the valley there are splendid views down Wharfedale towards Buckden.

pubs in both dales are amongst the finest in the area.

The walk described here is a little more ambitious and the fact that there are a couple of good pubs en route is purely fortuitous. In fact, it is a fairly demanding walk and if you want to stop at a pub (indeed, if you want to stop at all) you'd best make a whole day of it.

It begins in the enormous car park at Buckden from where the narrow motor road called Dubb's Lane is followed for a few hundred yards until a broad lane leads off on the left. This too is macadamed at first but it soon becomes a bridleway, gravelled like some country house drive. Originally this route over Old Cote Moor Top was a corpse road along which bodies were taken for burial at Arncliffe in Littondale, there being no burial ground in upper Wharfedale. Later, a smelt mill was built on the moor just above the village and no doubt that helped to improve access for the first half mile or so. The lane climbs steadily up the hill, with views back towards the village.

The quality doesn't last for long. At a signpost a peat path leaves the road and begins its boggy ascent of the moor. Tall posts are stuck at intervals along the way, presumably to mark the path, though it isn't too difficult to follow. Here and there gritstone flags appear under foot, but mostly it is hard going on soft peat, though the inclination isn't steep and the distance not excessive; perhaps a couple of miles to the top.

When the angle does finally ease off completely, by some decrepit walls, a trig block can be spied just a few minutes walk to the left. This is the official summit of Old Cote Moor (607m, 1992ft)—official because there are at least two other places on the moor marginally higher but totally unmarked! They are also inaccessible, so we'd best settle for what we've got.

The route now plunges down into Littondale 'as straight as a beggar can spit', to use Kipling's graphic phrase. Boggy at first, it soon improves and then, where the valley sides suddenly steepen, it becomes a slanting rake of luscious grass—a truly green, green lane. This seems to have always been a feature of the green lanes at Litton, where grazing on the highway used to be let on an annual basis. The lane crosses the end of Crystal Beck, a deep and mysterious-looking ravine, to finish directly at the Queen's Arms, which has been a pub since 1842 and a very good one, too.

Now the walk crosses the river and for a couple of miles travels along the flat valley bottom to Halton Gill Bridge, where the narrow motor road from Stainforth drops down off the fells to the valley.

Halton Gill was something of a crossroads in the old packhorse days. Tracks from it went to Horton and Settle in one direction and via the Horse Head Pass to Hawes, Bainbridge and Middleham in the other. Eventually the Settle Road and the Bishopdale road were

Halton Gill, the start of the Horse Head Pass.

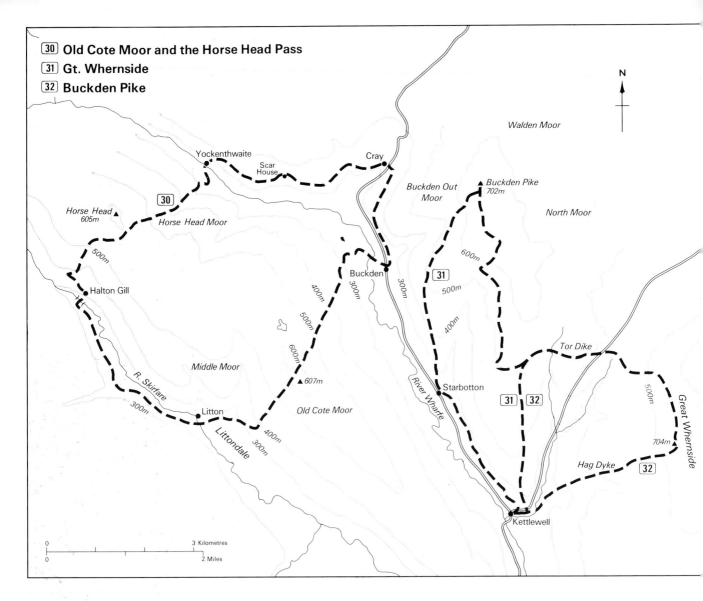

surfaced, but the link between the two, the Horse Head Pass, never was. It remains very much as it was in the old days and it makes a grand crossing of the fells.

It begins at a gate just beyond the last house of the village and climbs as a broad stony highway up the moorside. As it does so it reveals wonderful views down Littondale and across to Fountains Fell and Pen-y-ghent. The hamlet of Foxup, tucked away in its little dell at the head of Littondale seems particularly idyllic on a fine summer's day.

Horse Head Gate is a gap in the wall which runs along the top of the moor and represents the summit of the Pass. Away to the left, just a few minutes's walk, can be seen a trig block which marks the summit of the moor, Horse Head (605m, 1985ft). The name 'Horse' is a

corruption of 'hause', a gap. From the Gate it is all downhill to Yockenthwaite, fairly steeply and on a path which has deteriorated from what it was on the other side. It traverses the edge of a limestone ravine, Raisgill, and from about halfway down offers superb views across to Buckden Pike and the Yockenthwaite Moors, with the hamlet of Yockenthwaite itself looking like something from a picture postcard.

The path eventually joins the narrow motor road which travels through Langstrothdale to Hawes, just a few minutes from Yockenthwaite. Here the old packhorse bridge, shaded by sycamores, gives access to the village green and the very imposing farmhouse built in Georgian times with a high walled garden and recessed stone summer house, like something

120

from Chatsworth. The path we want goes round the back of the farm and is well signposted. It leads up onto a limestone shelf which contours round the head of the valley all the way to Cray.

There is often no path to speak of along this stretch of the walk, so you need to keep a sharp eye open for the squeeze stiles and the little footbridge across Strans Gill, a deep slot in the limestone, reminiscent of Hell Gill in Mallerstang, though much smaller. Old buildings, barns which were probably once farms in their own right, and are now ruinous, litter the landscape until the only farm still occupied appears, half hidden by trees. This is Scar House, an early Quaker meeting place, where George Fox came in 1652 and 1677 full of missionary zeal. The Quakers had a burial ground here.

After Scar House the walk becomes, if anything, even more wildly romantic. Trees and limestone blend together and there are superb views down Wharfedale to Buckden and beyond. At Crook Gill, even the moors look attractive, seen through the rift made by the gill.

At last the path descends through a farm to the White Lion at Cray, the second pub on our route and strategically placed to offer us refreshment for the last couple of miles. The route goes through the ford opposite the pub then up the fell a little way by a less than obvious path, to the green lane that is Buckden Rake. The Rake is really a continuation of the green lane that travels over Stake Pass to Raydale and is part of the ancient Roman road from Bainbridge to Ilkley. It traverses round, high above the valley floor, until at last it descends majestically to Buckden—straight into the car park.

Scar House was an early Quaker meeting place.

WALK 31: Great Whernside

Map: Yorkshire Dales Western Area, 1:25,000.
Start: National Park car park in Kettlewell, MR971723.
Distance: 7 miles.
Time: 3½ hours.
What's it Like?: A very satisfying mountain ascent—perhaps the best outside the Three Peaks area. Steep, approximately 500m of brutally direct ascent. An interesting descent along Tor Dike with some excellent views of Wharfedale.

Note: As with Buckden Pike (See Walk 32) there are no rights of way shown on the top part of this fell but the way described has long been in customary use.

Connections with Other Walks: This walk can be combined with the ascent of Buckden Pike, the union taking place at the junction of the green lanes Starbotton Road and Top Mere Road.

Shorter Alternative: Climb to Hag Dike then return along Dowber Gill Beck. 3 miles, but quite a climb.

Bad Weather Alternative: Down the valley is Grassington, with a museum, park centre and bookshops.

The Most Easterly Mountain in the Pennines

Because we measure mountains by their height it always causes surprise that Great Whernside, above Kettlewell in Wharfedale, is 32m lower than its humbler namesake in the Three Peaks. Great Whernside doesn't have the shapely appearance of its namesake either, yet it is bigger in area, and it is probably this that earns it its title. Certainly it feels every inch a mountain when you are climbing it; a graceful

Hag Dike, the lonely farmhouse now used by Scouts as an outdoor pursuits centre.

ascent matched only by Ingleborough, in my opinion.

It is said to be the most easterly mountain in the Pennines (counting a mountain as 2000ft+) and its name refers to grindstones made from the millstone grit which forms the mountain's summit. There is much more evidence here of millstone grit, lying naked and rough to the winds, than on the Ribblehead Whernside, so perhaps the 'Great' comes from that too!

The walk starts in Kettlewell alongside the beck which flows through the village. Tarmac gives way to a broad track until at a stream junction a signpost points to Hag Dike and we set off on a very steep ascent up a long spur of fellside. The path was obviously well made at one time but the gradient is such that it could never have seen a cart; only mules could have gone that way, perhaps servicing some of the ancient bell pits in the area.

As height is gained there are views across to Old Cote Moor and Buckden Pike, whilst nearer to hand is the deep rift of Dowber Gill Beck with its impressive little valley head. The spoil heaps of the old Providence Lead Mine can be seen there, and there is a well known cave too, Providence Pot, which has a through passage to Dow Cave, a mile to the north, in the next valley.

Up ahead there is a crest of rough fell littered with gritstone scree and topped by a series of cairns as if in competition with Nine Standards Rigg. These are our markers, because the path all but disappears and the mountain top has not been in sight for some time. Climbing up towards these, the way suddenly reveals a substantial farmhouse tucked into a fold of the fell. This is Hag Dike, as lonely a place as one could wish for and long since abandoned as a farm. Nowadays it is an outdoors pursuits centre for Scouts.

The path passes through the yard of the building and then climbs stonily up to the cairns, from where the final ascent can be seen. At first it is less steep, though boggy, then it climbs straight up to the top, exactly to the trig block. All round is a jumble of enormous gritstone boulders and slabs, extremely rough in texture (704m, 2310ft).

The top of Great Whernside is an elongated plateau running roughly north and south for about a mile, though only a quarter mile wide. Our way follows it north—there is no path to speak of—with views over the east side to the wild moors of Nidderdale and the Scar House and Angram reservoirs. At Black Dike End a wall comes up the western side of the fell and there is a narrow path down by the side of it which leads to a stile and a very steep path down to Hunters Sleets, the summit of the motor road from Kettlewell to Coverdale.

At right angles to the road and topped by a dry stone wall, is an ancient defensive ditch known as Tor Dike, which was part of the fortifications erected by the rebel Brigantes

Below left: **The walk begins and ends in the charming village of Kettlewell.**

Below right: **The summit of Great Whernside.**

against the Romans. Venutius, leader of the rebels, constructed a military base at Stanwick near Scotch Corner and this ditch at Tor Dike was meant to protect his southern flank. The Romans attacked in AD74 and Venutius was defeated.

The direct route to Tor Mere Top and Buckden Pike from Hunters Sleets is not open to public access and there are notices posted to that effect on the moors. Instead, our route follows the path along the top of Tor Dike until it meets the substantial green lane of Starbotton Road. This contours round, dropping slightly and giving remarkably fine views down Wharfedale, until a signpost is met at a junction in the lane, with one finger pointing to Starbotton and the other to Kettlewell.

The Kettlewell lane, called Top Mere Road, is green at first, then stony and walled. With unerring swiftness, for it is steep and straight, the lane leads back to Kettlewell and the car.

Storm clouds over Kettlewell. In the background, right, is Great Whernside.

WALK 32: Buckden Pike

Ruined walls on the ascent of
Buckden Pike.

Map: Yorkshire Dales Central Area, 1:25,000.
Start: National Park car park in Kettlewell,
MR971723.
Distance: 9 miles.
Time: 5 hours.
What's it Like?: A long and elegant approach,
giving a good taste of the old and famous green
lanes above the valley. The summit walk is very
boggy. The return is logical and very fine but
does need some good map reading.
Connections with Other Walks: 1) The
Great Whernside walk (Walk 31) can be continued over Buckden Pike before descent to
Kettlewell. About 7 hours.
Shorter Alternative: Walk to Starbotton along
the river by the Dales Way then return by the
path described in the text. Nice little valley walk
of about 4 miles.
Bad Weather Alternative: Retire to
Grassington or further still to Skipton where
there is a fine castle, interesting museum,
working corn mills and forges and other educa-
tional wonders.

The Memorial Cross and Buckden Gavel

Buckden Pike rises directly above the village of
the same name at the head of Wharfedale. It is
an isolated sort of mountain, separated by
deep cols from Great Whernside on the one
hand and Yockenthwaite Moor on the other,
and shapely too, in a modest way, like a great
jelly mould.

As with a number of other peaks hereabouts, there are no rights of way on the top of
Buckden Pike, though of course, the mountain
has long been climbed by all and sundry,
usually by the direct path from Buckden Rake.

Above left: **Buckden Pike.**

Above: **The mining level at Buckden Gill.**

A more interesting walk, however, can be got from Kettlewell by starting up the Top Mere Road green lane which is used for descent in Walk 31. This means that strong walkers can combine Great Whernside and Buckden Pike into one outing, should they so wish.

The lane starts from a sharp right bend near the bottom of the motor road from Kettlewell to Coverdale and climbs straight up the fellside, first as a rocky bridleway between walls, then as a grassy lane to the junction with the Starbotton Road, another green lane. From this position there are outstanding views down Wharfedale and, nearer to hand, the intriguing earthworks of Tor Dike, built by the Brigantes as defences against the Romans.

Starbotton Road is a well-made packhorse track and by following it west for a few minutes, another junction is reached. One branch goes swiftly downhill to the hamlet of Starbotton, and the other traverses round the large side valley of Cam Gill Beck, climbing slightly. Here the road has deteriorated rather badly, being interrupted by patches of bog. It passes some old waste tips from lead mining and then, at the head of the gill, it joins yet another packhorse track, the Walden Road, which crosses the moors from Starbotton to Walden Head.

The number and quality of the packhorse routes hereabouts shows how important these moorland crossings were in the old days, both for lead and for wool. Fountains Abbey, Bolton Priory and Coverham Abbey all held land at Kettlewell, which was the regional centre and much more important than Grassington. On the track we are following, just before we reach the ridge, there is the ruin of a building which might have been a shelter for packmen. At the ridge there is a boundary stone marked B + O—the O probably being a mistake for C, since the stone marks the boundary of Buckden and Carlton Highdale.

Whatever your impressions might have been of the boggy state of the highway recently travelled, the next three quarters of a mile is going to make it seem like the M1. Prepare to meet thy bog—wet, muddy, interminable and inescapable—as you crawl up to the top of Buckden Pike. I am not an advocate of walking in wellies (though I once did the Three Peaks in them) but I could make an exception in this case. The good old Lancashire word *slutch* is the only adequate description of the conditions.

There is no path and the way is simple—just follow the wall. After a short distance you come to a memorial cross, standing forlornly in the bog. It commemorates five Polish airmen who were killed in the war when their plane crashed here. The effigy of a fox's head, fixed to the base of the cross, was put there by the sole survivor who crawled through the snow with a broken leg, guided to safety by following the footprints of a fox. He reckoned the fox would be going to a farm for food, and he was right.

You feel like Christian in the Slough of

Despond as you make your way towards the summit but at last there is a ladder stile leading over the wall to the trig block and adjacent substantial cairn (702m, 2303ft). For some reason the summit area is known as Buckden Gavel and perhaps at one time the name applied to the whole mountain for there are references to lead ore from 'Buckden Gavel', which obviously refer to the mine much lower down.

At the top a signpost points firmly to Buckden, but that is not the way we want to go. We want to go to Starbotton, which is in the opposite direction, and there is a perfectly good track which will take us there, except that access to it is barred by a wall. But a few yards back along the approach route, where this wall meets the boundary wall, there is a semblance of a stile—or at least the through-stones stick out in such a manner as to suggest a stile! There's even a pole to help you over.

Once over the wall a decent path leads across the moor and then steeply down into the ravine of Buckden Gill. The view of the village far below, framed by the steep walls of the gill,

is quite dramatic. At the head of the gill lie the remains of the Buckden lead mine. These too are quite dramatic, especially the portals of the adit.

A curious anomaly now arises. The path down from the summit is not a right of way, but is obviously well used, whereas the path from the mine to Starbotton *is* a right of way, but seems hardly used at all! It slopes in a long raking slant across the fellside, difficult to follow, needing good map reading, until it joins the broad green lane of the Walden Road, here deeply rutted. The lane tips steeply down a spur into the village. All the way down from the mine there have been excellent views.

Starbotton is an attractive old-world village, so typical of Wharfedale. There was once a smelt mill here, but it is hard to imagine industry in a place so idyllic. We walk through the village to the far side where a signpost points out a field path to Kettlewell. It is a superb end to the walk, partly wooded, partly open and with hardly any gradient. It is two miles to Kettlewell and the car.

Starbotton.

WALK 33: How Stean and Dale Edge

Map: Yorkshire Dales Central Area, 1:25,000. A detailed map of the gorge and caves is available in the café for a few pence.
Start: How Stean Gorge Café car park (marked Cat Hole on the map), MR094735. (NB. The car park is only for customer use—if you do not intend to visit the gorge, it would be preferable to start and finish in Middlesmoor [see text]).
Distance: 10 miles.
Time: 5 hours plus an hour to explore the gorge and cave.
What's it Like?: A walk with some wonderfully wide-ranging views. It rises and falls a mere 1000ft in ten miles, so it isn't strenuous. Except at the start and finish the walking is almost entirely on bridle ways or their equivalent, and very easy to follow. Under conditions of snow this would be a splendid winter outing for experienced walkers.

The gorge is quite separate but should not be missed. The combination of gorge and cave, so accessible to the general public, is probably unique in Britain.
Shorter Alternative: Follow the road to Stean hamlet, then a bridleway to Well House farm, cross the How Stean Beck at a ford (do not attempt it if the water is high—there's a bridge a few yards downstream), then by field paths to Middlesmoor. Follow a path to Northside Head and How Gill Plantation, then descend to Limley Farm, cross the River Nidd (here dry—it has gone underground) and soon join Thrope Lane back to Lofthouse and Stean. About 5 miles.
Bad Weather Alternatives: Ripon, Knaresborough and Harrogate are not too far away and each town has a wealth of interest.

There are extensive views of Nidderdale from the Dale Edge path.

A Walk in Remote Nidderdale

Nidderdale can fairly claim to be the forgotten valley of the Yorkshire Dales, unjustly neglected by walkers and National Park alike. Above Pateley Bridge, the large village at the entrance to the upper dale, the valley is wide and lush with trees and meadowland. But higher up still, beyond Ramsgill and Lofthouse, the great gritstone moors begin to throw dark shadows across the landscape. Though the dale bottoms may still be idyllic, those moors are as sombre and untamed as any you are likely to see.

In recent years the dale has been made more accessible to tourists because the waterworks road to the dam at Scar House has been opened and the road over the moors from Lofthouse to Masham has been surfaced, but even so, compared with neighbouring Wharfedale, the number of visitors is small. There is still this sense of isolation—almost of entrapment—and though there are plenty of good paths to follow, few of them lead out of the dale to give a wider perspective or show Nidderdale's place in the scheme of things.

And yet it remains one of the most beautiful of the dales. Why was it left out of the National Park, I wonder? Did all those reservoirs and grouse moors have something to do with it? It doesn't seem to affect the walking, thank goodness, and the route about to be described takes in the best of the upper dale.

It begins in the car park of the How Stean Gorge Café, because nobody should visit Nidderdale without sampling the Victorian splendours of the gorge. It is the sort of thing our forefathers delighted in: a deep, narrow, limestone gorge carved out by the How Stean Beck, with romantic walkways along dizzy ledges, protected by handrails, and footbridges spanning the chasm from side to side. There's even a genuine pothole to explore, though for this a torch is needed. It is called Tom Taylor's Cave after a highwayman who is supposed to have holed up there and it is entered from the gorge by steps, to emerge 530ft later—in the middle of the car park! In 1868 thirty-two Roman coins were found on a ledge in the cave by two lads, so you never know your luck. There are several other potholes at How Stean, and in Nidderdale generally, and though many are technically easy for experienced cavers they are best not entered by the inexperienced.

There's a charge for entry to the gorge, but you get free use of the car park for the day and the café is a good one.

The first part of the walk leaves the gorge car park and follows the road towards Stean for a few minutes until a signpost points the way to Middlesmoor. A delightful footpath descends to the beck where a bridge spans the chasm, for even here the How Stean carves out a deep gorge. Then the path, which is barely discernible, climbs the slopes towards Middlesmoor; a hamlet perched high above the junction of the Nidd and How Stean Beck.

Middlesmoor is an attractive place of handsome stone houses, a friendly pub and a church all huddled together, separated by narrow alleys. From the churchyard there is a celebrated view of Nidderdale—an extensive panorama funnelling away towards Pateley Bridge, and an almost equally impressive view up the dale towards Masham Moor. It is worth remembering these views of lush Nidderdale and contrasting them with what lies ahead—no other dale has such starkly contrasting scenery.

From Middlesmoor a long bridle path called In Moor Lane travels north-east, climbing

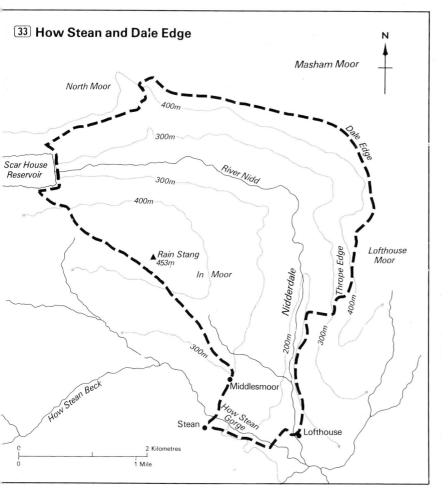

33 How Stean and Dale Edge

N

Masham Moor

North Moor

400m

300m

Scar House Reservoir

300m

River Nidd

400m

Dale Edge

Rain Stang 453m

In Moor

Nidderdale

Thrope Edge

400m

Lofthouse Moor

300m

200m

300m

How Stean Beck

300m

Middlesmoor

How Stean Gorge

Stean

Lofthouse

0   2 Kilometres

0   1 Mile

gradually the while. It is a stony road leading through a barren wilderness where in late August the heather lies in thick purple swathes stretching to the horizon. Grouse butts abound and there is even a trig block called Rain Stang (453m) just off the lane, though the real summit is a rounded rise of 495m about half a mile further on. It is quite distinctive.

From the lane the utter wilderness which surrounds Nidderdale on all sides becomes apparent. A circle of high fells sweeps round from Great Haw in the north to Little Whernside, Great Whernside and Meugher in the west. Between the summits are rolling moors stretching endlessly away, thickly clad in bracken and heather. The thought of walking such difficult terrain makes you feel more kindly disposed towards the stony lane you are on—not that you have any right of way off the track. The moors are strictly for the birds!

Two miles out from Middlesmoor the lane tips over a sharp edge and descends towards the Scar House Reservoir. A dam holds the water back; a stone dam with crenellated turrets which looks like a film set for the *Dambusters*. Is this why the RAF fly low sorties over here? Are they reliving past glories?

There's a road across the dam and raised platforms which give goods views down the dale. You can look down, too, on the associated buildings which lie below the face of the dam and admire the craftsmanship which went into the whole project. There is nothing cheap or shoddy about the Scar House dam; good Yorkshire stone carefully crafted and looking very handsome indeed.

From the dam too, you can see the route to be followed. The left-hand edge of the dale curves away, almost uniform in height, to a distant neb of fellside. This distinct skyline is known quite simply as Dale Edge, and there is a good path right round it.

It begins by climbing up from the dam until it meets the strangely named Woo Gill; a deep ravine with a tumbling beck. A minute later and a companion stream happily called Twiz-

The view of Nidderdale from Middlesmoor church.

130

Dale Edge begins at the attractive
Woo Gill.

131

Evening light on the reservoir and distant fells – the view back from Dale Edge.

ling Gill comes bubbling down to join the other, and then the path climbs up to the moor again. I suspect there has been some neglect of the right of way here, for the obvious route is not that shown on the map but one which follows a well-made track to an old shooting cabin before joining once and for all the Dale Edge path.

The Dale Edge path is seldom less than a bridleway in width, sometimes with the remnants of limestone cobbles, sometimes a grassy highway. It is a place for swift striding and glorious views. Every half mile or so the scene changes in the dale below. Only on the heights are the acres of heather unrelenting.

Eventually the path leads to an attractive shooting cabin, backed by a dark plantation of fir trees, like a scene from Hansel and Gretel. A faint path descends the steep fellside from here towards Thrope Farm in the dale bottom; one of the ancient abbey granges enjoyed by both Fountains and Byland in this dale. It is an attractive descent with fine views back to Dale Edge.

From Thrope Farm it is just a question of getting back to the car. There is a field path climbing to Middlesmoor and a reversal of the morning's start; or a path by the river which has nothing to recommend it and is soon pushed out onto the road; or Thrope Lane which can be followed to Lofthouse, where there is a narrow footbridge over the Nidd leading to the Stean Road. There's not much to choose between them and they each take about half an hour to reach the How Stean Gorge Café car park.

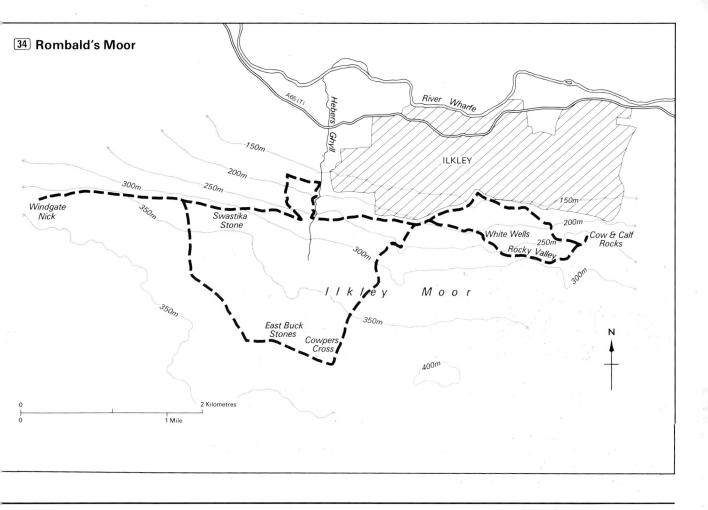

WALK 34: Rombald's Moor

Map: The best map for walking on the moor is produced by the West Riding R.A. *Ilkley Moor*, 1:25,000. Obtainable from the local Information Centre, opposite the railway station.

Start: Suitable parking exists below White Wells and at the Cow and Calf (MR130469). There is a large pay car park in the centre of town, too. Ilkley is accessible by metro rail from Bradford—from the station walk up Wells Road to the start, about 5 minutes.

Distance: 10 miles.

Time: 5 hours.

What's it Like?: An unusual moorland walk, quite unlike anything else in this book. From Cow and Calf to Heber's Ghyll you will meet all the world and his wife, from the Ghyll to Windgate Nick far fewer walkers and on the upper moor, practically nobody. A unique experience, especially if combined with a walk round the town itself, which is full of Victorian charm.

Shorter Alternatives: There are many alternatives but one which still incorporates much of interest is to follow the itinerary as far as the Swastika Stone, then return from there by Silver Well Cottage (about 5 miles).

Bad Weather Alternatives: Visit the information centre opposite the station where there is advice and pamphlets about what to see in the town.

On Ilkley Moor Baht 'at

Rombald's Moor is a great stretch of upland south of Skipton, separating Airedale and Wharfedale. Nobody seems quite sure who Rombald was; some say he was Robert de Romille, first Norman lord of Skipton, and

that the moor should be Romille's Moor, whilst others say the name goes further back to an early Christian saint, St Rumold. Yet others link the name with a mythological giant whose chief sport was hurling boulders all over the place—boulders for which the moor is now renowned. Certainly there are plenty of them: boulders and small crags litter the moor in great profusion, many of them carved with ancient symbols, especially the cup-and-ring marks (a hollow surrounded by rings carved out of the rock) similar to those found in many other parts of the world. An old guidebook lists no fewer than 35 such rocks on the moor and the local Information Centre has a guide pamphlet to help you find the most important of them.

The key to all this wonderland is the charming little town of Ilkley which still retains all the grandeur of a minor Victorian spa. The first hydropathic hotel in the country—hence the word hydro—was built here in 1844, and called Ben Rhydding. Hydropathy was a treatment for gout and other ailments which consisted mainly of cold baths and vigorous exercise and appealed to the Victorian sense of moral righteousness. It was so successful that by the 1890s there were fourteen others.

However, it was neither its popularity as a spa, nor its archaeological treasures, which brought undying fame to the moor, but a song written by a Lincolnshire clergyman in Victo-

rian times. Ilkley Moor is that part of Rombald's Moor which lies above the town, and *On Ilkley Moor baht 'at* has become one of the best-loved folk songs in the English language.

The walk which follows takes in some of the best-known landmarks of Rombald's Moor. Many of these happen to be on Ilkley Moor, within easy reach of the town, where all the world and his wife (not to mention the dog) are to be found on any reasonably sunny day. Further out, however, it is different; this can be a lonely moor, too. The walk starts from Wells Road, where the edge of the moor meets the town.

From the roadside a path leads up to a sort of rustic shelter and beyond it to The Tarn, tamed like the pond in any public park, but with a backdrop of high gritstone crags such as no park has ever seen. The paths are braided through sheer popularity, but they lead encouragingly towards the crags, over a tumbling beck. Then they veer away to the left to reach the Cow and Calf rocks, as incongruous a natural phenomenon as you are likely to see in a month of Sundays.

The Cow is a minor but bulky gritstone cliff, and the Calf is an immense boulder lying below it—said to be the largest free-standing boulder in England, though I wouldn't like to compare it with the Bowder Stone in Borrowdale in this respect. It looks a little careworn, perhaps

was a third rock—Bull Rock—but that it was broken up and used for roadstone, probably early in the last century. Round the back of the Cow lies Ilkley Quarry; a popular playground for climbers.

Our route climbs over the top of the Cow rocks, then below the gritstone edge which forms Rocky Valley; six impressive buttresses about fifty feet in height, separated by steep grass slopes. The path winds along below these, over hummocky ground, and the rocks, the slope of the moor and the distant prospect of Ilkley makes an enchanting scene.

The path eventually drops down to a compact cottage known as White Wells—appropriately painted, and the most conspicuous thing on the moor when seen from Ilkley. At the week ends the cottage offers refreshments, but it is also a museum and the original bathhouse of Ilkley, built by Squire Middleton at the end of the 18th century. The bath still exists and can be viewed; it is beautifully made.

An unsurfaced road goes steeply down from the bathhouse to a small car park below, but before that is reached there is a less well-used track veering off to the left and keeping more or less the same height across the moor. It meets a metalled road in half a mile, then a stream which it crosses by a little footbridge and continues in a westerly direction just above the fringe of Victorian villas which marks the edge of town. The hydros are no more, of course—that sort of treatment fell out of favour many years ago—but some have been converted into retirement homes, hotels and even a college of further education. Some, alas, have been destroyed, including the original Ben Rhydding.

From the footbridge the path is clearly defined, being a popular excursion for all and sundry. In half a mile it passes a little reservoir and just beyond this there is an old kissing gate giving access to the woods on the right. Through the gate a path plunges steeply down a wooded ravine known as Heber's Ghyll, crossing and recrossing the stream by little footbridges in a perfect expression of Victorian romanticism. What with the woods and the ferns and the burbling beck, it is the archetypal fairy glen so beloved by our forefathers.

The path through the glen meets a surfaced road eventually. This runs along the edge of the woods until a path leaves it and skirting the last fringe of trees climbs back up to the moor. Up above there is a rocky promontory of black gritstone, Woodhouse Crag, crowned by an

because it is treated as a gymnasium by climbers, but also because the surroundings are worn thin by curiosity seekers like ourselves. There's a set of steps cut up the back of the Calf so that the daring can make an ascent if they feel bold enough.

Local traditions has it that at one time there

enclosure of iron railings like some forgotten family vault. It is only a matter of minutes to climb up to the top of the rocks and see that the railings protect one of Ilkley's best-known archeological treasures, the Swastika Stone.

The wind and rain of centuries have worn away the stone so that the ancient symbol is barely legibile anymore. A perfect replica has been cut and put in front of the original so that visitors can see what a marvellous piece of art it is. The swastika has since the dawn of time been an Aryan good-luck symbol, but this is no ordinary swastika. Its crooked arms melt into sinuous curves, suggesting procreation, or the life force itself.

Beyond the Swastika Stone the path runs straight and clear along the edge of the moor for two miles to Windgate Nick, where the moor turns a corner and offers views of the west and east sides which until now have been unseen by the walker. The nick is just what its name implies, of course—a distinct gap in the moor's edge where an old path comes up from the valley and runs away again to Airedale. Such nicks are fairly common in the northern hill country.

Windgate Nick is the outermost limit of our walk. We now have to return along the moorland edge until a right of way can be found which will lead us onto the upper moor. There is such a path, but it is not easy to find or follow. It starts about a mile back from the Nick in a small walled enclosure, but the path is non-existent and the stile, probably through lack of use, is in a bad state of repair.

As you tackle this problem you can see that Ilkley Moor is really a series of shallow steps and that what you have been walking along thus far is the edge of the first step. Now you tackle the next step, not steep or high, but with only the faintest trace of a path to help. Once this is conquered a broad moor stretches away in front of you towards a third edge where there are some conspicuous rocks, the East Buck Stones, acres of planted conifers and a telecommunications mast. In autumn the moor

The bleak heart of Rombald's Moor with East Buck Stones.

Rombald's moor near Windgate Nick; a quiet part of the moor.

is one great blanket of purple heather where the grouse whirr and squawk with startling suddenness from beneath your feet.

The path becomes good for a bit, past old boundary stones, then loses itself in the only stretch of bog on the entire walk. It's a relief to tackle the slopes up to the rocks which turn out to be not nearly as impressive as they seemed from a distance. Nearly all gritstone crags have this quality of seeming imposing from a distance, only to be much less so on closer acquaintance.

Above the rocks there is a wall and this guides you towards the telecommunications mast where, quite suddenly, a road appears. On the far side of the wall, where the road runs up to the mast, it is surfaced and one fondly imagines at first that it is a modern access road, but it turns out to be nothing of the sort. It is a very old road from Ilkley to Keighley and as you follow it across the moor towards the former town, you can see places where the old surface is still intact, probably from the 18th and 19th centuries. The road itself is older than that—perhaps even Roman—and a little way down it there is an ancient cross known as Cowper's Cross, whose origin is lost in time.

As you walk along the road back to Ilkley you can gaze at the wilderness all about and wonder how the War Office could once envisage such a place as a military depot. Yet in 1872 they had plans to station up to 100,000 men on the moor, with railway lines climbing up from Bingley and Guiseley and even a canal to transport heavy goods like cannons! Fortunately, the locals objected so strongly that the plan was dropped. One can only imagine that some military commander in Whitehall had read about Venutius camping out on Ingleborough during Roman times!

The road leads down swiftly to the town and the car.

137

WALK 35: Fountains Abbey and Studley Royal

Map: The best map for this walk can be purchased for a few pence from the National Trust shop near the entrance to the estate. Called *Fountains Abbey and Studley Royal, Yorkshire*, it is essential for the proper identification of the many points of interest.

Start: Large car park (pay) near the west entrance, MR270681. There is a charge for entering the Abbey and park.

Distance: 2½ miles.

Time: Allow 3 hours minimum. At popular times there are free guided tours of the Abbey and, separately, the gardens.

What's it like?: A fascinating and unique walk of great loveliness. Choose a sunny day in spring or autumn for maximum effect and fewest visitors. This place is very, very popular—one of the great tourist sights of Britain. The walking is easy throughout on good paths; trainers are ample. A torch might be useful in the tunnel (see text)—small children can find it quite scary.

Shorter Alternative: The walk can be shortened in many obvious ways. Shortest of all is just to visit the ruins.

Bad Weather Alternative: 1) Fountains Hall is not without interest; 2) The city of Ripon is nearby and worth exploring.

Ancient Ruins in a Romantic Landscape

Was there ever a more romantic setting for a ruin than that of Fountains Abbey in the vale of the little River Skell? The river is scarcely more than a stream (a *skell* is a fountain, incidentally, and hence the name) but it has carved out a quiet dale, now well wooded, whose banks seem almost to embrace the great monastery with its tall North Tower and traceried windows. On a fine evening the

The gardens and the canal at Studley Royal, with the Moon Pond and Octagon Tower.

St Mary's church stands on the hill beyond the Lake. Next to it is the obelisk erected in 1805 in memory of John Aislabie.

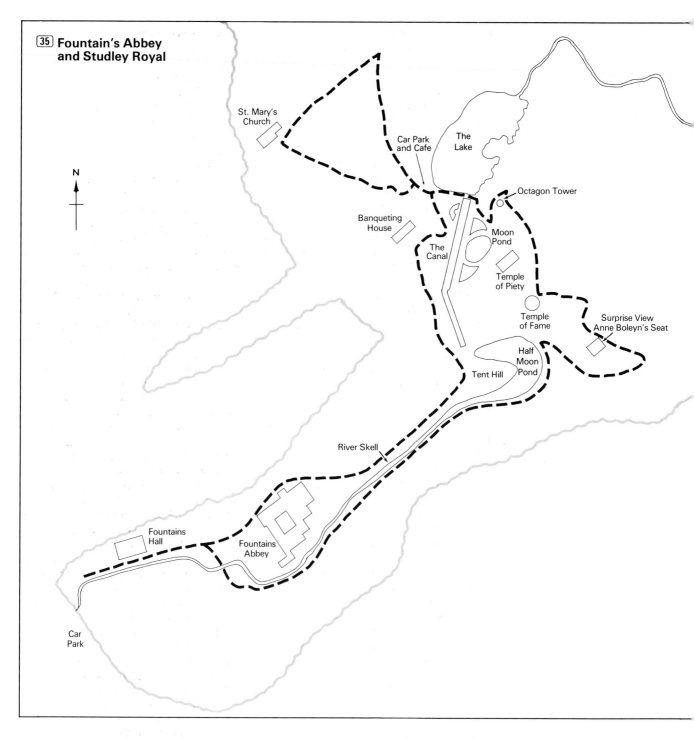

35 Fountain's Abbey and Studley Royal

broken sandstone walls glow in the setting sun and the whole effect is breathtaking.

These magnificent ruins would be worth a visit on their own account, but they would scarcely qualify for inclusion in this book were it not for Studley Royal, the classic 18th-century park or 'pleasure garden' created by the Aislabie family beyond the Abbey. Now

the ruins and the park are in the care of the National Trust and together they make a short walk of unusual beauty and interest, suitable for the entire family.

The walk follows the River Skell from west to east along its northern bank and returns on the south. There is excellent car parking because on high days and holidays Fountains

140

is very popular indeed and if it is solitude you are seeking this is not the place for you. Across the road from the car park a broad drive leads towards the abbey but before the ruins come into view there is a fine Jacobean manor house, Fountains Hall, built by Sir Stephen Proctor in 1611 with stone taken from the Abbey. It is open to the public.

Soon the drive opens out onto a broad greensward beyond which the ruins of the Abbey rise in all their splendour. In its heyday, before the Dissolution of the Monasteries, Fountains was one of the richest and largest abbeys in England, a Cistercian foundation of 1132. Destroyed by fire in 1140 it was rebuilt between 1150 and 1250, though the fine North Tower, which is such a striking feature of the ruins, was not added until the early 16th century. When complete, the Abbey buildings extended over some 12 acres, of which about one sixth is occupied by the present remains.

The Abbey was handed over to the King in 1540 and sold to Sir Richard Gresham who subsequently disposed of it to Stephen Proctor who dismantled the Abbot's Lodgings and Infirmary to build his fine house. Subsequently the ruins passed through various hands until they were acquired by William Aislabie and joined to his estate of Studley Royal.

The question facing a walker on his first visit is whether to explore the Abbey first, then do the walk, or complete the walk, leaving the rest of the time to explore the Abbey. The second is the more logical but quite impossible to achieve—who could possibly resist those fantastic ruins? They draw like a magnet and before you know what's what you are embroiled in discovery, lost in the grandiose architecture. In season there are free guided tours to the ruins at regular intervals and these take about an hour—done on your own, guidebook in hand, it scarcely takes less if you are to make sense of what you see around you. On the other hand, sense may not be what you want; there are those who feel it is enough to soak up the spirit of the place, to wonder at the majesty of the ruins, the skill of the old monks and what I have called elsewhere, the Ozymandias effect. This place saw Rome tremble.

On the north side of the abbey a broad and surfaced bridleway leads below sandstone bluffs through some narrow parkland to a curious man-made hill called Tent Hill which was thrown up during the construction of the pleasure gardens at Studley Royal. It served two purposes: to act as a backcloth to the great canal which John Aislabie had made—and to prevent his neighbour from looking over into the garden! Later on, of course, the Aislabies acquired Fountains, so the second consideration no longer applied.

Around the foot of the hill stretches the Half Moon Pond, made by widening the river, and beyond it the remarkable gardens of Studley Royal. The first sight is so unexpected—even though you may be aware of their existence—that you stop and blink.

These are not gardens as we know them today, nor is the park anything like the municipal variety. It is landscaping on a broad canvas; the achieving of formal informality; the marrying of rigidly designed canals, yew hedges, trimmed lawns and geometric ponds with wooded hillsides, tumbling in apparent natural confusion. It is Versailles on a small scale–and yet not quite; there is something very English about this scene.

John Aislabie inherited the estate in 1699. He was Chancellor of the Exchequer at the time of the unfortunate South Sea Bubble which ruined so many prominent men and for a short time he was held in the Tower on a charge of corruption. He got off lightly, for none of his property was seized. His career was shattered, however, so Aislabie retired to his Yorkshire estate and made the creation of the Studley gardens his life work.

Work had already begun in 1716 but now it was carried on in earnest. The main gardens had been finished by 1730 and two years later construction of the various buildings began. When John Aislabie died in 1742 the work had been completed but it was left to his son William to add the jewel in the crown by purchasing Fountains Abbey in 1768. In the late 18th and 19th centuries there was little alteration or additions, and so Studley Royal presents a perfectly preserved classical garden, beautifully restored to pristine condition by the National Trust.

The footpath continues along the north side of the river, now canalised. Across the water can be seen the Moon Pond and formal grass walks beyond which is the classic Temple of Piety and high up, amongst the trees, the Octagon Tower. On the left, hidden by trees, is the lovely little Banqueting House.

Before long the path leads to the East Gate beyond which is the large lake and the great Deer Park. There is also another car park and café, for this is an alternative way into the gardens. The water cascades from the canal into the lake and up on the left is the spire of St Mary's Church, built 1871–78, at the west end

Far left: **Fountains Abbey.**

Left: **The Octagon Tower is one of the many delightful buildings in Studley Royal park.**

The ruined grandeur of Fountains Abbey.

of a magnificent avenue of limes and sweet chestnut which runs east-west from the main entrance of the estate. Built in the style of the 14th century the church is reputed to have cost £50,000 and is lavishly embellished. The imposing spire, which can be seen for miles around, is 152ft high.

From the church it is possible to spend some time exploring the Deer Park, but our way leads back to the Cascades at the end of the Canal, where stepping stones lead across to the other side. The National Trust have supplemented the stepping stones with a footbridge, which seems a pity, but no doubt they have safety in mind. Such cosseting seems endemic today.

The return leg of the walk is rich in the Romantic follies of the 18th century—perhaps the finest such collection of any garden in England. The footpath leads by the round Moon Pond and the lead statues of Bacchus, Neptune and Endymion to the classical Temple of Piety, built in Doric style and dedicated originally to Hercules. Recently restored, the Temple is not open to the public.

Nearby a path climbs up through the woods towards the Octagon Tower but before that building is reached there is an outcrop of rock into which a staircase has been cut—leading nowhere, as was usual with these Romantic follies. Opposite, there is a ruined arch leading to a rock bower, but the *piece de resistance* is the long subterranean passage—the only way of reaching the Tower. Because it bends, the tunnel is quite dark and full of mysterious sounds like dripping water and ghostly echoes. Little wonder that some young children find

Autumn at Fountains Abbey.

the tunnel frightening.

The Tower is not open to the public, but from nearby there is an impressive view across the vale to the Banqueting Hall in its wooded bower.

A high-level path goes through the trees past a small rotunda known as the Temple of Fame and on to a little summerhouse known as Anne Boleyn's seat and Surprise View. And surprise there is—a stunning view of the ruins in all their glory.

From Surprise View the path descends steeply to the Half Moon Pond and then follows the bank of the river until at the ruins it starts to climb again, though only slightly. It seems to me that in recent years the trees have become thicker on this rise, obscuring the Abbey to some extent, but in spring there are wild cherry petals blowing in the wind and perhaps enough gaps to glimpse the ruins and the river. Soon the track breaks cover, descends the hill and crosses the Green towards a bridge over the stream. There is a café and toilets here, but also, by the bridge, is the place to get one of the best of all the many views of Fountains Abbey. It is a fitting climax to a grand little walk.